BECOMING

a CHURCH *that*
CARES WELL *for*
THE ABUSED

BECOMING
a CHURCH *that*
CARES WELL *for*
THE ABUSED

handbook

BRAD HAMBRICK, *General Editor*

churchcares.com

B&H PUBLISHING
NASHVILLE, TENNESSEE

978-1-5359-8814-8

Published by B&H Publishing Group
Nashville, Tennessee

Dewey Decimal Classification: 362.82
Subject Heading: OFFENSES AGAINST THE PERSON / CHURCH
WORK WITH THE ABUSED / PSYCHOLOGICAL ABUSE

Cover design by Jason Thacker.
Cover photo by Carolyn V on Unsplash.

2 3 4 5 6 7 8 • 23 22 21 20 19

To survivors who have courageously told
their devastating stories.

To victims who need to know they will be believed
and cared for when they come forward.

To advocates who have faithfully served as God's
heralds, calling the church to repent of her failures
in this area, and who also long for change.

We hope this project honors your suffering,
courage, and faithfulness.

We pray this work assists the church to become
the refuge God intended His people to be.

Contents

Knowledge does not make hard things easy. But knowledge can make confusing things clearer. If you have been involved in abusive relationships, whether that be personally or ministerially, you know that *nothing with abuse is easy*. Our goal in this training is to make your role as a pastor or ministry leader clearer.

At the end of this training you should be able to say, "I know *what* I should do when there is a report of abuse in my ministry, *why* I should do it, and *how* to do it." From there it is your responsibility as both a citizen and Christian to have the integrity and courage to take action as one of God's agents of protection for those being harmed or oppressed by various forms of abuse.

PART ONE
Key Concepts *for* Pastors and Ministry Leaders

Lesson 1 – Ministry Context: The Church's Response to Abuse Is Grounded in the Gospel   3

Lesson 2 – Ministry Tension: Matthew 18 Complements (Doesn't Compete with) Romans 13   17

Lesson 3 – Ministry Responsibilities: Abuse Against a Minor vs. Abuse Against an Adult   31

Lesson 4 – Ministry Partners: Awareness of Key Professionals in Victim Advocate Roles   45

PART TWO
Key Responses *from* Pastors and Ministry Leaders

Lesson 5 – Key Responses to Sexual Abuse   63

Lesson 6 – Key Responses to Physical Abuse   77

Lesson 7 – What Happens When You Call CPS? Don't Avoid
What You Don't Understand   93

Lesson 8 – Non-Criminal Forms of Abuse (Verbal and Emotional) 107

Lesson 9 – Pastoral Care After Reporting: Reporting Is *Not*
a Ministerial Hand Off   121

Lesson 10 – Pastoral Care and Correction for an Abuser   137

Lesson 11 – Response to Abuse by a Church Leader   153

Lesson 12 – Seven Next Steps after this Training   169

Appendix A   181

Appendix B   243

This training experience is designed to include both this handbook and video resources. The accompanying videos for this handbook and other supplemental resources can be found at **churchcares.com**.

Contributors

BRAD HAMBRICK

Pastoral Counselor and Seminary Professor

Brad Hambrick serves as the Pastor of Counseling at The Summit Church in Durham, North Carolina. He also serves as Instructor of Biblical Counseling at Southeastern Baptist Theological Seminary, a council member of the Biblical Counseling Coalition. Brad's background in pastoral care and creating resources for churches served to shape the educational design for *Becoming a Church that Cares Well for the Abused.*

RACHAEL DENHOLLANDER

Survivor, Advocate, Attorney

Rachael Denhollander is a sexual abuse survivor, advocate, attorney, and educator who became internationally known as the first woman to file a police report and speak publicly against USA Gymnastics team doctor Larry Nassar, one of the most prolific sexual abusers in recorded history. As a result of her activism, over 250 women came forward as survivors of Nassar's abuse, leading to his life imprisonment. Rachael and her husband Jacob live in Louisville, Kentucky, with their four young children.

DIANE LANGBERG
Psychologist

Diane Langberg (PhD) is a globally recognized psychologist, known for her forty-five years of clinical work with trauma victims. She has trained caregivers on six continents in responding to trauma and to the abuse of power. She has authored several books and directs her own counseling practice in Jenkintown, Pennsylvania, Diane Langberg, PhD & Associates.

ANDREA MUNFORD
Police Lieutenant

Andrea Munford is a lieutenant with the Michigan State University Police Department. Lieutenant Munford was formerly assigned as the Investigative Division Commander and was the department's primary investigator for the MSU PD Special Victims Unit (SVU). During that time, Lieutenant Munford was the lead investigator for the Larry Nassar case. Lieutenant Munford is currently assigned as the training coordinator for the MSU PD Center for Trauma Informed Investigative Excellence.

MIKA EDMONDSON
Pastor

Mika Edmondson, a native of Nashville, Tennessee, is the pastor of New City Fellowship. He graduated from Calvin Theological Seminary, where he wrote a dissertation on Martin Luther King Jr.'s theology of suffering. He is happily married and has two beautiful daughters.

LESLIE VERNICK
Speaker, Author, and Relationship Coach

Leslie Vernick was a licensed clinical social worker in private practice for over thirty years, working with individuals and couples in destructive and abusive relationships. She is the author of seven books and is currently a national speaker, blogger, and relationship coach.

KARLA SIU
Social Worker

Karla Siu is a Licensed Clinical Social Worker with more than eighteen years of experience serving families and children recovering from trauma. Karla currently provides consultation to the North Carolina Farmworker Health Program and El Futuro, Inc. to implement bilingual video-counseling services in select primary care clinics in rural North Carolina. Formerly, Karla served as an outpatient therapist and El Futuro's Clinical Program Director for eleven years. Karla also worked in welfare reform, community mental health, research on biculturalism, and services to domestic violence offenders. In 2009, Karla coauthored an article in the *Journal of Family Violence*.

DARBY STRICKLAND
Counselor and Instructor at CCEF

Darby Strickland (MDiv) is an instructor and counselor with the Christian Counseling & Educational Foundation. She teaches Counseling Abusive Marriages, and her writing and speaking focuses on training churches to care well for those affected by domestic abuse.

CHRIS MOLES
Pastor and Batterer Interventionist

Rev. Chris Moles is an ordained minister with the Christian and Missionary Alliance, the Senior Pastor of Grace Community Chapel in Eleanor, West Virginia, and a Certified Biblical Counselor (ACBC and IABC). Chris is also the author of the book *The Heart of Domestic Abuse: Gospel Solutions for Men Who Use Violence and Control in the Home*. A certified group facilitator in batterer intervention and prevention, Chris has served as a faculty member with the West Virginia Coalition Against Domestic Violence statewide intervention training. He holds a BA in Bible from Cedarville College and a MA in Biblical Counseling from Faith Bible Seminary.

SAMANTHA KILPATRICK
Attorney

Samantha Kilpatrick is an attorney with over twenty years experience in the practice of law. She is currently a partner with Kilpatrick Law Group, PLLC in Raleigh, North Carolina. She is a former prosecutor with experience in the areas of domestic violence and sexual assault crimes. Currently in private practice, she represents and counsels survivors of abuse and advises faith-based organizations on abuse prevention, policy, and safety.

PART ONE

Key Concepts *for* Pastors and Ministry Leaders

Ministry Context: The Church's Response to Abuse Is Grounded in the Gospel

Do you remember what was on the forefront of your mind when you began ministry? In Luke 4, we get to see what was on the forefront of Jesus' mind.

> He came to Nazareth, where he had been brought up. As usual, he entered the synagogue on the Sabbath day and stood up to read. The scroll of the prophet Isaiah [chapter 61] was given to him, and unrolling the scroll, and he found the place where it was written,
>
> > "The Spirit of the Lord is on me, because he has anointed me to preach good news to the poor. He has sent me *to proclaim release to the captives* and recovery of sight to the blind, *to set free the oppressed*, to proclaim the year of the Lord's favor."
>
> He then rolled up the scroll, gave it back to the attendant, and sat down. And the eyes of everyone in the synagogue were fixed

on him. He began by saying to them, "Today as you listen, this Scripture has been fulfilled." (Luke 4:16–21, emphasis added)

Jesus was clear. His ministry would change the lives of the captive and oppressed. While He certainly meant this on a spiritual level (meaning that every person is in desperate need of freedom from sin and death), Jesus also cared about oppression in a physical and relational sense.

Spiritual oppression and captivity are conditions that *all* of us are born into, but we must not forget that these things are experienced by many at a relational level as well. The "captive and oppressed," in our day, must include not only those who are in spiritual bondage to sin, but also those who live in fear of physical abuse in their homes or churches, those who are raped, those who are preyed upon as minors, and others like them.

Jesus' half-brother James clearly understood this message. He said true Christianity must care for the weakest and most vulnerable in our communities. When churches fail to do this or become complicit in the harm, James would say we have become "stained by the world" (James 1:27), marked by very the things we are called to change.

On one hand, it is easy to think of abuse as just a social issue. If we do, we will think better laws, better law enforcement, more shelters, or more preventative campaigns are the remedy for abuse.

These things are good. Christians should fully cooperate with and be involved in these areas because abuse *is* a social issue. But it's not *just* a social issue. When we think of abuse as solely a social issue, then the church is not the refuge for the oppressed that God intended His people to be.

On the other hand, it may be equally tempting to think that if the church's response to abuse is grounded in the gospel, then we merely want people to repent of their sinful episodes of abuse. As Christians, we want every sinner to repent. There is no greater hope.

But this approach misses the severity of violation and coercion captured in the word *abuse*. If we are naïve to this reality, then instead of being shepherds who protect God's children, we can easily and unintentionally become part of the problem, prioritizing the wrong initial responses.

So what do we mean when we say, "The church's response to abuse is grounded in the gospel"? To answer this question we must realize that the gospel invites *the sinner* to *find forgiveness in Christ through repentance and it also invites* *the sufferer* *to find refuge in the Comforter from a harsh, broken world where things like abuse occur.*

The reality is that *we are all both sinners and sufferers.* But with some struggles our moral agency is at the forefront. That's when sin is there. With other struggles the moral agency of others is in the forefront. That's when suffering is the forefront struggle.

With abuse, our ministry priorities should be: first, remove the opportunity for further damage, and second, to address the sin that creates the damage. After all, this is what we would do for one of our children.

MINISTRY REFLECTION

Based on your ministry training and experience, do you feel more skilled in working with anger or grief, adultery or miscarriage, gossip or depression? What does your answer reveal about how much your ministry has emphasized the implications of the gospel for sin as compared to suffering? Which do you think your ministry leans toward?

_____

_____

_____

_____

Historically, the church has been more skilled in applying the gospel to sin than suffering. Hence, in pastoral care, we ask relatively few non-moral questions about abuse. To the degree we get involved, we focus on getting the destructive person to simply stop their abusive actions more than: (a) assessing the safety of the victim, (b) evaluating whether a criminal act took place, or (c) helping the victim understand the impact of being abused.

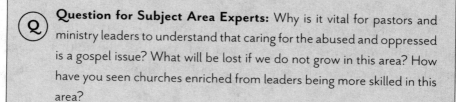

HEAR FROM THE EXPERTS

Q **Question for Subject Area Experts:** Why is it vital for pastors and ministry leaders to understand that caring for the abused and oppressed is a gospel issue? What will be lost if we do not grow in this area? How have you seen churches enriched from leaders being more skilled in this area?

A **Answers from Subject Area Experts:** Watch the experts' responses at churchcares.com, under the Video Training section, in the video entitled: *Lesson 1 – Ministry Context: The Church's Response to Abuse Is Grounded in the Gospel.*

Leslie Vernick: I'm reminded of the verse in Ecclesiastes 4 where it says, "Again I looked and saw all the oppression that was taking place under the sun: I saw the tears of the oppressed—and they have no comforter; power was on the side of their oppressors—and they have no comforter." Luke's gospel brings us the good news us that Jesus came to bring light to those who sit in darkness, to those who are oppressed. To those who are hopeless and forsaken. Jesus shows us what God's kingdom is like (John 1). God's kingdom shows the power of love. The world's kingdom rests on the love of power. The very heart of abuse is centered in the love and misuse of power. Pastors and ministry leaders must recognize this misuse of power whether it's in the church, the community, or the family, as well as speak up and help those oppressed by it. By doing this, we do demonstrate the merciful heart of God to those who have been harmed.

Rachael Denhollander: The gospel means "good news." It is meant to bring hope and freedom and redemption. And the people who cry out the most for the very things the gospel is supposed to bring, are those who have suffered the opposite—hopelessness, imprisoned in their abuse, violated, and left to feel unredeemable. Abuse takes every concept we need to understand the gospel—things like love, trust, sacrifice—and redefines it to be a weapon for doing great evil. As ministry leaders, your job is to bring this good news to your flock. In order to do this, you must understand how abusers operate and what they damage, and you must know how to apply the good news to this damage in a way that really makes it "good news."

Karla Siu: Over the years of counseling abuse survivors, I've learned to run back to the gospel often. Especially because abuse often leads to confusion and an overwhelming sense of hopelessness. In this returning to Jesus' work on the cross, I've experienced the power of God anew each time. It's clear to me now that the gospel is essential to caring for the abused and oppressed because it is the very power of God for salvation as Romans 1:16 says. The gospel reveals how Christ's work on the cross reversed death once and for all. This good news is the basis for our hope, and is what allows us to offer the very same hope and purpose to those we are ministering to who have experienced abuse, just as 2 Corinthians 1:3–4 affirms.

Mika Edmondson: We simply cannot talk about the historical reality of the cross without speaking of abuse. The Romans stripped and deliberately hung victims of crucifixion naked in order to humiliate them, to add emotional distress to their physical agony. When Christ submitted Himself to this experience at the cross, He made abuse a gospel issue. It was part of the oppression that He bore at His cross and overcame at the resurrection. So when we fail to recognize various forms of abuse as "gospel issues" we lose an important aspect of the freedom Christ has won for us. He came to reveal God's great hatred of abuse and His great love for the victims of it. As pastors, we must help God's people understand the solidarity, empathy, and deliverance that His risen Son holds out to victims of abuse. In Christ, they have a savior who understands exactly what they are going through because He has been there Himself.

Darby Strickland: We need to remember that God delivers His people not just from their own sin but also from injustices. When God speaks to Moses out of the burning bush, He says "I am the God of your fathers, I have observed the misery of my people, I have heard their cry on account of their oppressors. I know their sufferings, and I have come down to deliver them." God introduces Himself to His people as their deliverer and protector. God asks His people repeatedly in Scripture to work for justice and righteousness. This is who we, as worshippers of God, are told to be, people who do justice. God calls us to confront oppression but also to provide protection and care for the vulnerable. We see Jesus doing these things. He identifies with the powerless, takes up their cause, and stands against those who do harm to the vulnerable. This is who we are to be, deliverers and protectors.

Samantha Kilpatrick: As an attorney and advocate, justice is a word I use often, but it seems to get lost in the response to abuse. We must view the gospel as more than just forgiveness. The gospel goes deeper and wider. It is about salvation, but also about day-to-day living—about hope and justice. Proverbs 31:8 has guided my work; it urges us to "Speak up for those who have no voice; seek justice for those on the verge of destruction."

We serve a Savior who brings light into dark places—abuse is a dark place, a place where Satan can thrive by multiplying shame and doubt. We bring light—the gospel—to these places by prioritizing the suffering of victims, by validating their stories and the sin that has been perpetrated against them, and by being a refuge and safe haven.

Andrea Munford: In law enforcement, we often quote Proverbs 28:1, "The wicked flee when no man pursueth: but the righteous are bold as a lion" (KJV).

Much like ministry care, those in police work choose that profession because they feel a calling to serve those who are abused, oppressed, ignored, or afraid. Police work is God's work. In the Holman Christian Standard's *Police Officer's Bible,* the commentator tells us, "God created three institutions: the family, the church, and the government . . . and part of the mission of government is to restrain evil." Romans 13:1–2 tells us, "Everyone must submit to the governing authorities, for there is no authority except God, and those that exist are instituted by God. So then, the one who resists authority is opposing God's command, and those who oppose it will bring judgment on themselves" (HCSB). When someone abuses or oppresses another in so committing a crime, law enforcement officers are the investigators that hold offenders accountable and protect those who have been harmed.

Diane Langberg: When we fail to serve the abused and oppressed, we fail to follow our Head. A body that does not follow its head is a sick body. When we turn from those who have been abused—in our midst or elsewhere—we have chosen to value something else more than love and obedience to our God. We are called by God to care for those who are afflicted and needy; to tend broken hearts and to release the captives. Such Christ-like work not only brings hope and healing to the abused. Our loving obedience to God in this arena is also transformative in our lives as we become more like Jesus Christ.

Chris Moles: Because people are made in the image of God, abuse in all its forms represent demonic distortions of God's clear design for people and relationships. It's past time that we (the church) follow God's clear mandate to care for the oppressed and to lovingly and humbly confront and correct oppressors. The church can become a safer place for the vulnerable, and a place where abusive people will not be allowed to continue their abuse. Isaiah 1:17 says, "Learn to do good; seek justice, correct oppression; bring justice to the fatherless, plead the widow's cause" (ESV).

———————

Why are we more skilled at addressing sin than suffering? It is usually not because we lack compassion, but because we do not like feeling out of control and we lack training. When we minister to those who are suffering, we're often not sure what to tell them to do next. We feel powerless and ignorant. This study will take us deep into areas where we do not have control and for which ministry leaders need more training.

HEAR FROM THE EXPERTS

Q **Question for Subject Area Experts:** How do you maintain hope when your vocation has you perpetually in situations where the most important things that need to happen are outside of your control?

A **Answers from Subject Area Experts:** Watch the experts' responses at churchcares.com, under the Video Training section, in the video entitled: *Lesson 1 – Ministry Context: The Church's Response to Abuse Is Grounded in the Gospel.*

Chris Moles: Early on in the work I would become discouraged when a guy remained obstinate or didn't change fast enough, or fully enough for my taste. I needed to shift my focus to becoming like the farmer in Jesus' story who sowed seed everywhere. I deliver the message, I entreat when necessary, I give the process everything I have, but I now measure success by faithfulness. If he repents, praise the Lord, we can be faithful to continue discipleship, observe the fruit of repentance, apply proper consequences, etc., And if he remains obstinate, then we can practice the full extent of church discipline, applying pressure to oppressive person while properly caring for the victim. Either way reaching a conclusion for the sake of the victim that is hope giving.

We have to admit that often our systems and processes have left victims suffering while we try and "figure this out." I think our past failures as well as the complexity of this work has led me to value and rely heavily on team ministry. I try to fulfill a very specific role (abuser education and accountability) and enlist as many competent team members as I can to help. I've often said this is an "all hands on deck" kind of work. I want to encourage you in much the same way that Jethro said to Moses in Exodus 18: Pastor, ministry leader, "The work is too heavy for you; you cannot handle it alone" (NIV). Partnering with competent counselors, advocates, law enforcement, and other experts positions you to do your best work and to care well for everyone involved.

Diane Langberg: Some years ago I began to see my work as an invitation from God into the fellowship of His sufferings. I realized I will never encounter anything that He has not borne. He came in the flesh and entered into and bore our darkness, alone, forsaken. He who is light has invited me to enter some of that darkness *with Him* as my constant companion. There He teaches both those I care for and me, transforming both sides as we walk together. I am called to obedience in His ways. The ultimate outcome I am learning to leave with Him. He has also taught me that if I am to endure and not get twisted by the darkness, I need two things. One, of course, is to stay very close to Him and live in obedience to Him. Two, I am a frail and finite human and must pursue the antidote for the poison I encounter in this world. That antidote is beauty—His beauty found in this world He created. For me, these very human antidotes are found in the beauty of the natural world, in music, in good friends, and in family. These are the human things that nourish and replenish me as I continue on with this work grounded in hope.

What do we do when we feel out of control? We usually change the way we engage the situation in order to give ourselves a greater sense of control. As the following examples show, we miss the underlying issues of power and control, leaving the abused vulnerable.

- We focus on the parts of the situation we understand best and seem most open to change (the garden variety elements in the struggle) so that we feel more competent. "It sounds to me like you guys need to think about how you handle your schedules since your most explosive conflict is about the challenges related to your children's activity calendars."
- We interact with the parts of the conflict we know what to do with as God's top priority because we want to regain our grip on a situation that is starting to feel slippery. "I can tell how much respect means to you and it sounds like it is becoming an idol. The most important part of any life struggle is to make sure that God is in first place in your life."
- We focus on the failings of the most cooperative person in the room (the abused) because they'll respond favorably to our instruction. Tragically, this comes out as something like, "I think we can get some traction towards things improving if we work on how you respond when your husband is upset."

MINISTRY REFLECTION

When you feel incompetent in ministry settings, what are your characteristic patterns of trying to regain control? What are your tendencies in high conflict situations? We need to know these patterns because they will emerge in the care of abused individuals. What we don't acknowledge in ourselves will hurt those God has called us to shepherd.

_____

_____

_____

_____

_____

At this point, it's probably clear that caring for the abused is grounded in the gospel for another reason—God is going to use our role in caring for others to force us to come to grips with our *own* weakness, which should push us to greater reliance on Him. We will come to learn 2 Corinthians 12:9, "God's grace is sufficient. God's power is made perfect in weakness," as Paul learned it and as victims of abuse learn it, in our weakness.

I want to challenge you to engage honestly and fully with this study. Allow it to help you wrestle with these topics, even as they are uncomfortable, complicated, and painful. Pray that you would become more "comfortable being uncomfortable," so that in the moments this study is needed, you will be a grounded anchor for a soul being tossed and battered by the waves of abuse in the moments they need you most.

HEAR FROM THE EXPERTS

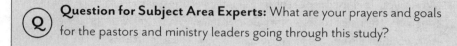

Question for Subject Area Experts: What are your prayers and goals for the pastors and ministry leaders going through this study?

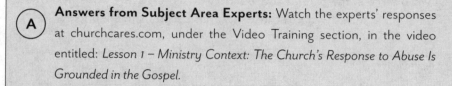

Answers from Subject Area Experts: Watch the experts' responses at churchcares.com, under the Video Training section, in the video entitled: *Lesson 1 – Ministry Context: The Church's Response to Abuse Is Grounded in the Gospel.*

Rachael Denhollander: As you go through this course, my prayer for you is that the depth and beauty of the gospel is made increasingly more real, and that you begin to both feel the enormous weight of ministering to the wounded, and also the incredible hope you can be equipped to bring.

Leslie Vernick: I remember when a client of mine first told me that she had been sexually abused by her father when she was a child. I knew him. He attended my church and I felt afraid. I wasn't sure what to do next and I didn't want to do the wrong thing. Do I believe her? Do I confront him? Do I call the police? Who can I ask about what to do with what she told me? You don't get this roadmap in seminary or graduate school, but this course will give you that roadmap with clear biblical principles that will help you with your overwhelm, your confusion, your fear, and your next steps forward.

Darby Strickland: I have come alongside many pastors who are ministering to those affected by abuse. They are overwhelmed and often filled with sorrow for what they didn't know or perceive. It is my prayer that this training prevents this from being your experience. This curriculum blesses you with a biblical map, serving as a guide for the most disorienting situations so that you are able to wisely care for your sheep.

Chris Moles: Pastor, ministry leader, I love you and I'm praying for you and your team as you walk through this material. I'd encourage you to approach these lessons with a teachable spirit and a humble heart. Some things may be new, or hard to hear, or overwhelming, but it's worth wrestling with. You are so needed in this work; with your help we can truly see the church become the safest place on planet earth.

Samantha Kilpatrick: My prayer for you as pastors and ministry leaders is that through this study you will realize the great responsibility of protecting your church and others from predators and seek out ways to prevent, educate, and detect evil in your midst. I pray that you will see these circumstances as divine opportunities to walk alongside a hurting brother or sister. I pray that those who confide in you will leave with more hope than when they came—feeling believed, validated, and protected.

Mika Edmondson: My prayer is that God will grant each and every pastor going through this study the grace to "weep with those who weep." To take the burdens and sorrows of God's hurting people onto themselves to the point of shedding tears with them, to truly reflect the heart of Christ toward them, and to firmly resolve to do what it takes to practically care for them.

Diane Langberg: My hope is that you will follow *your* Shepherd and listen and learn so you might care for the sheep entrusted to you—many of whom are afflicted and needy and tossed aside, remaining silent and untended.

Andrea Munford: I pray for church leaders to develop a deeper understanding of trauma and its effect on victims of abuse, and to develop relationships with law enforcement and community resources so that you can walk beside people in pain without judgment, but with the love in the ministry role God has placed you in.

Karla Siu: My prayer for you is that you are able to persevere in the hope that we have in Christ, however dark and dismal a situation may appear. I pray that we remain rooted in this true hope . . . "bearing fruit in every good work and increasing in the knowledge of God" (Col. 1:10 ESV).

KEY POINTS OF THIS LESSON

- The church's care for abuse is grounded in the gospel because one key aspect of Jesus' ministry was freedom and healing for the oppressed.
- Being an accurate ambassador of Christ and shepherd of his people means being as skilled in ministering to suffering as dealing with sin.
- As ministry leaders, we need to be self-aware about how we wrongly reframe uncomfortable situations to regain a false sense of control.

FOLLOW UP RESOURCES

- Article: "We Are Equally Sinful. We Are Not All Equally Broken or Toxic," by Brad Hambrick; http://bradhambrick.com /we-are-equally-sinful-we-are-not-all-equally-broken-or-toxic/

- Article: "Counseling Triage: Where to Begin with Complex Struggles" by Brad Hambrick; http://bradhambrick.com/triage2/

- Podcast: "Protecting the Vulnerable," with Julie Lowe; https:// www.ccef.org/podcast/protecting-vulnerable-julie-lowe/

Ministry Tension: Matthew 18 Complements (Doesn't Compete with) Romans 13

When you hand a surgeon a blade, they think "scalpel." When you hand a fisherman a blade, they think "filet." When you hand a chef a blade, they think "julienne." While the shape of the knife should make it obvious what it is for, you get the point—the role of a person impacts how he or she interprets a situation.

This is no less true for pastors and ministry leaders. When people come to us with various problems in living, we assume their struggle has a church-based answer. After all, why else would they come to us?

Actually, there is a logical answer. Victims of abuse often come to church leaders with life struggles that, at least in part, are legal matters for one simple reason: *trust*. They feel safe with us. Being abused is disorienting. Talking to a stranger about abuse is even more unsettling. Often abuse victims talk to church leaders first because of a pre-existing relationship of trust. *We want to be a good steward of that trust.*

HEAR FROM THE EXPERTS

 Question for Subject Area Experts: Describe the frame of mind and thought processes that are common when an adult or minor is preparing to make their initial disclosure of an experience of abuse. Revealing abuse can as traumatic as the experience of abuse; if this is true, why do victims often choose to reveal abuse to church leaders?

 Answers from Subject Area Experts: Watch the experts' responses at churchcares.com, under the Video Training section, in the video entitled: *Lesson 2 – Ministry Tension: Matthew 18 Complements (Doesn't Compete with) Romans 13.*

Rachael Denhollander: In your role as a ministry leader, you are very likely to receive disclosures of abuse. This is because the victim desperately needs what you preach and promise. Surely, someone who understands holiness and sin, justice and perfect love, will understand the depth of the evil they have experienced.

This means that how you respond will become intertwined with the survivor's understanding of Christ and the gospel.

A victim who discloses to you is facing almost paralyzing fear and shame. The darkest, most intimate, private violations they never wanted anyone to see, they now have to speak out loud. They are also usually facing extreme self-doubt—many times victims have been so conditioned in the abuse that they question their own judgment, or think of abusive behaviors as "normal," when they aren't normal at all. Many times the trauma has resulted in memory gaps and the victim is keenly aware of everything that can be used to discredit them.

This means that when a victim discloses, they are unlikely to use words like *abuse*, and they are likely to minimize or downplay what they've experienced, often even only disclosing a small part of what has been going on to see if you are safe. What the victim has been through is almost certainly far worse than you will initially hear.

The lies a victim hears in her own mind—it's their fault, their shame, it's not that bad, they are overreacting—are so loud that if your response in any way reflects those lies, it is absolutely crushing. They are unlikely to speak to you again, they may even retract or soften their own allegations if your response indicates they are not safe and have not been believed. It often takes years for a victim to seek help after being crushed, even unintentionally.

Leslie Vernick: When a person voluntarily discloses to their pastor that they are being abused or have been abused, they feel terrified that you won't believe their story. And this can be especially true if you know the accused. It feels unbelievable, unthinkable, unimaginable. Your initial reaction may be: surely the abused has misunderstood, exaggerated things, or even made them up. And when disclosing, the abused may doubt what is really true, questioning am I overreacting? Is this normal? How could someone who says they love God or love me, do this? Did I deserve it? Maybe it is my fault.

Abuse is crazy making. It messes with a victim's mind because abusers are experts at deflecting responsibility and blaming their victims for their abuse. "If only you hadn't looked so pretty I wouldn't have done that," or "Why did you make me so angry? It's your fault I hit you."

In addition, abusers are people we know. They can be charming and likeable people. They aren't always abusive. They don't look like monsters. They look like us. And victims aren't always likeable or engaging individuals, and in their pain and trauma, may sound confused, contradictory, unbelievable, and sometimes mentally unstable.

Here's where you need to be very cautious. Listen hard, talk little. It can be tempting to focus your attention on what the victim may be doing that seems sinful, such as cursing, immodest attire, or having a hard or unforgiving heart.

Or you may want to ask the victim some questions that unintentionally blame him or her for being victimized. For example, when disclosing abuse in marriage, asking the victim, "What are you doing that makes your spouse so mad at you?" or after a victim discloses sexual assault asking, "Why did you go to that party, or not cry out for help?"

Studies show that abuse is traumatic, but disclosing abuse can be more traumatic when the victim isn't believed or blamed by those trusted to help.

You represent God to the victim who asks for your help and justice. *Does God care about what's happened to me?*

I know you want to represent Him well. And the best place to start is with compassion and care so that the victim feels heard, believed, and loved.

What might cause us to be a poor steward of an abuse victim's trust? Let's go back to the "parable of the blades," and remember the lesson: we see what we expect to see because of the role we are in.

As ministry leaders, when we hear *abuse* we tend to think "severe sin" (strong moral category) rather than "crime" (legal category). In an upcoming lesson, we will come back to this idea and wrestle with the question, "Is all abuse criminal and, if not, what do we do when severe relational dishonor is immoral and destructive but not illegal?" For now, let's keep things simple.

When we think about how to handle "severe sin," what passage of Scripture comes to mind? Chances are, one of the passages on our short list is Matthew 18. When a church member is being abusive, church discipline is an appropriate—even if neglected—response. We will talk more church discipline later in this lesson. But what happens when our first thought upon learning of abuse is Matthew 18? Without realizing it, we have selected one ministry path to the exclusion of others.

Most counseling mistakes do not happen because we ask the right questions and arrive at a wrong conclusion. Most counseling mistakes arise from the questions we don't ask and, therefore, never consider the possibilities that might need to occur. In abuse cases, when we think Matthew 18, we usually neglect considering Romans 13.

MINISTRY REFLECTION

Imagine someone comes to you for pastoral care. They disclose some combination of volatile conflict with a few episodes of physical violence; that their spouse is monitoring their communications and limiting their social relationships. What are your next ministry steps?

_____

_____

_____

_____

_____

Biblical steps sloppily taken don't provide safety. It is possible to hurt people with the best of intentions and good theology poorly applied. When "severe sin" is also "illegal," we need to understand how Romans 13 relates to Matthew 18 in order for Matthew 18 to be applied in a way that honors God's design for both passages.

Let's think about how these two passages relate to one another. First, we ask ourselves the question "Is it like God to assign different roles to different people in complex tasks?" Our answer is "yes." In the care of a congregation, God assigned different roles to deacons (Acts 6:1–7) and pastor-elders (Eph. 4:11–13) and the one-another ministry among church members (Gal. 6:2).

Now we ask, "Has God assigned different roles to different people in the specific complex task of caring for abuse victims?" Because most forms of abuse are illegal, we again find that the answer is "yes."

- In Romans 13 God assigns the governing authorities to run point on things that are *illegal*.
- In Matthew 18 God assigns the church to run point on things that are *immoral*.

It can feel awkward to differentiate immoral from illegal. The categories do overlap. For our purposes here, suffice it to say that abuse is always immoral and usually illegal.

HEAR FROM THE EXPERTS

Question for Subject Area Experts: What are common reasons why ministry leaders often miss the illegal in the immoral? Why is it unwise for the church to act as an investigative body in criminal matters? For what reasons have you seen churches been tempted to not report illegal and criminal acts?

Answers from Subject Area Experts: Watch the experts' responses at churchcares.com, under the Video Training section, in the video entitled: *Lesson 2 – Ministry Tension: Matthew 18 Complements (Doesn't Compete with) Romans 13.*

Mika Edmondson: As pastors, we must have the humility to recognize the limits of our own callings, competence, and pastoral jurisdiction. In situations of physical and sexual assault, although a sin has occurred, a crime has also been committed. We pastors are not trained to properly investigate crimes. With certain crimes, we intuitively understand this. If for instance, we found a murdered body on the floor of our pastoral study, we would immediately call the police. It would never occur to us to investigate the crime of murder completely "in house" because we recognize we are simply not called or equipped to properly do it. The same holds true for crimes like sexual and domestic abuse. Many dynamics in these situations require trained experts to address. The Lord's people are better protected and served when we leaders understand that. This should also come as a tremendous relief for pastors. We are called to walk with the Lord's people as they navigate these difficult issues, but we are not called to resolve them, to be legal, investigative, or judicial experts. We do tremendous damage when we think we are.

Sometimes church leaders also fail to report abuse when we are tempted to prioritize the reputation of the church over the well-being of individual victims. In a crisis, it seems much easier and safer to attempt to handle everything within the church rather than get the civil authorities involved. We are afraid of scandal and we often tell ourselves we are simply protecting the reputation, peace, unity, and interests of God's church. But when we fail to pursue justice using the best resources available, it doesn't protect our reputation. And it doesn't promote grace, peace, or unity. Victims are denied the grace of healing and restoration when their complex emotional scars are addressed by novices rather than experts. They are also denied protection and peace of mind as their abuser is often given more care and encouragement from the community than they received. The reputation and unity of the community becomes compromised when the church looks to the world as it is complicit in a cover up, uninterested in justice, and unconcerned for victims. Churches truly protect their reputation when they do the right thing and prioritize transparency and light, rather than secrecy and darkness.

Andrea Munford: We often listen to solve things instead of listening to understand, and we miss important factors because we process the information to come up with a solution. When we do that, we fail to recognize much of what victims of abuse are saying. Church leaders can often be focused on reconciliation, but they are typically not trained in recognizing trauma or potential safety issues. There can also be related crimes that aren't as apparent in a disclosure that may not be recognized by ministry leaders. This is where relationships with police and advocates are so important, to provide that expertise.

There have also been situations where church leaders do not report crimes because the offender is part of the church and they don't want to get them in trouble. This is not only problematic for victims, as it can add to their trauma, but it also poses risks to their safety and the safety of others. When a victim reports, or someone reports on their behalf, it can be the most dangerous time for them, as offenders sometimes retaliate against the victim, and sometimes this can be an act of violence. This can also create a danger to the entire church family, as abusive offenders can be unpredictable.

This also presents the problem that an offender may not be held accountable, therefore putting them in position to re-offend on the same victim or others.

———————————

All of this begs the question, "What do we, as ministry leaders, do when Romans 13 overlaps with Matthew 18? What do we do when there are *civil responsibilities* and *pastoral responsibilities* for the same people and events?" Even by asking the question this way, we are much more likely to arrive at a wise and good answer.

Here are at least five key priorities necessary to answer this question well:

1. *If civil authorities need to be involved, make sure they are notified.* We, ministry leaders, did not know we had a role until the victim had the courage to come to us. The same is true for the civil authorities.

2. *View civil authorities as complementary teammates who have the same initial objective: the safety of the victim(s).* The jurisdictional authority of a social worker or police officer can help promote safety in a way that a pastor, deacon, or small group leader cannot. We should be grateful for their involvement.

3. *Realize the legal process may delay some aspects of ministry involvement.* Church leaders can be frustrated when an attorney advises silence about the allegations until after a trial, when waiting on a series of hearings, or when a restraining order interferes with communication. However, these delays are not a reason to begin to view the civil authorities as a competitor in our pastoral care efforts.

4. *Seek to be an asset to the civil authorities.* When church leaders fulfill their role in notifying civil authorities, civil authorities are more prone to view church leaders as an asset to their work. Ask the simple, open-ended question, "How can we help?"

5. *Realize that even though the church's role is broader (redemptive) and longer (not just to the resolution of the legal concern), the input and expertise of the civil authorities can be very helpful to good pastoral care.* How civil authorities gauge the severity of an abuse case can be a very helpful reference point for a church. Churches do not have the same level of day-to-day experience with criminal acts compared to law enforcement, so we should seek to learn from their wisdom as we deal with abusers and victims.

HEAR FROM THE EXPERTS

 Question for Subject Area Experts: When church leaders interact with civil authorities, social workers, or mental health professionals, what common mistakes do you see in this process? What one or two things can a church do to stand out as most helpful in these instances?

 Answers from Subject Area Experts: Watch the experts' responses at churchcares.com, under the Video Training section, in the video entitled: *Lesson 2 – Ministry Tension: Matthew 18 Complements (Doesn't Compete with) Romans 13.*

Chris Moles: Among the most profitable experiences for myself as a pastor has been connecting and serving alongside community-based agencies. Partnering with other professionals in this work will not only sharpen your skills as a people helper,: it will free you to function best as a member of the team, saving you valuable time and energy. More partnerships means more eyes on the problem and more wisdom around the table, as well as, opening future doors for kingdom expansion and ministry engagement. We just never know, in the moment, how the connections we make will lead to the redemption of others or our own sanctification.

Samantha Kilpatrick: In my experience, churches make mistakes when they try to handle everything in-house. This is problematic because churches are not equipped in all of the proficiency needed in an abuse situation. Church leaders are often hesitant to get the "government" involved—usually due to mistrust, coupled with a desire to handle abuse internally. Rather than mistrust, the church should view these authorities as a resource—God-ordained entities that have been put in place for the safety of those they serve and protect.

Two helpful things a church could do to make these interactions more productive are to learn about the agencies that respond to abuse and build relationships with individuals who work in these areas.

In most states, reports of child abuse are handled by an entity like Child Protective Services or CPS. Generally, CPS exists to intervene and protect in situations where a child is being harmed or neglected by a parent, guardian, or caretaker. CPS does not investigate in order to criminally prosecute an offender. While CPS and the police are not the same, they often work in cooperation with one another.

On the other hand, law enforcement agencies (the police) handle reports of abuse that are criminal involving adults and children. The criminal justice system runs completely independent of the child protective system. Local police departments and district attorney's offices are charged with enforcing criminal laws in order to protect the public and to punish offenders.

The most proactive thing a church can do is build relationships with individuals in these agencies before a crisis arises. Reach out and find out about your county child protective services office—look for ways your church can serve that agency, invite someone to come train on child abuse and reporting. Get to know local law enforcement. Have an officer come to your church and do a walk-through and discuss crisis planning. Make a connection with someone in the district attorney's office, as well as, a lawyer in the community that can answer these types of questions. Build relationships that will allow you to ask questions and get help during a crisis.

Karla Siu: There are two things that stand as most helpful as church leaders seek to interact with civil authorities and the broader professional community.

1. You'll have to be both persistent and patient. I always encourage new social workers to remember that many of our systems are working at or beyond capacity. It will require grace and persistence to break through, even when you have a strong relationship with other helping professionals. There's

the temptation to give up if you have called a few times with no immediate response, but I learned over time that it was rarely a straight-out-dismissal of my request, and more that my colleagues were juggling various crises, not just the one I was reaching out to them about. Tips for bridging this very real barrier are to remain flexible and extend grace whenever possible.

2. It is important to start our conversations with our civil authorities and the broader professional community in a spirit of mutual respect and collaboration. As Christians, we can work well together—and will need to—work with people who may not share our beliefs. Missionaries are often working alongside "persons of peace" who may not share in their convictions and beliefs, but who are willing to provide support, care, etc., in a foreign context. Similarly, you may encounter more oft than not, that secular settings may and often are used by God to bring about the healing and care for the wounded members of our congregations.

Most of this lesson has been about how Romans 13 relates to Matthew 18. We've looked at how church and state should cooperate. Now we'll consider how *churches* can cooperate with one another. Matthew 18 helps us see how one church should relate to another church. Too often, when church discipline doesn't end in restoration, abusers leave a congregation, and the prior church *fails to warn the next church of predictable danger.*

Why is it that churches fail to notify other churches of church discipline cases? Answers can range from poor record-keeping to willfully choosing to protect the abuser. In many cases it's prompted by a fear of litigation. A more formal documentation and structured process are needed to ensure communication happens in a liability-reducing and ministry-effective manner.

We have provided you with a sample documentation process for church discipline in the follow up resource section. You will notice two features of this documentation system that are relevant to this discussion:

1. Early in the process, the member is asked to *sign a release of information,* not for permission to conduct discipline (membership in a church already includes this), but to allow the church to communicate with everyone beneficial to holistic pastoral care and to share progress notes with a new church if discipline does not result in restoration.
2. The history gathering, actions steps, and level of cooperation from the member under discipline *are documented in such a way that the new church can have an accurate history* of what transpired under your care.

For instances of non-criminal abuse which would not show up on a background check but would be pertinent to a new church vetting someone for membership, these steps can save another congregation immense heartache. It also makes our restorative care efforts more likely to be successful.

MINISTRY REFLECTION

Imagine a guest seeks to become a member of your church, and also seems eager to serve on leadership levels. You contact their former church and learn they left while under an incomplete church discipline attempt. That church sends you a well-organized history of the discipline process like the one in the follow up resource section. In how many ways would this bless and protect your church?

_____

_____

_____

_____

_____

KEY POINTS OF THIS LESSON

- In Romans 13 God assigns the government to run point on things that are illegal.
- In Matthew 18 God assigns the church to run point on things that are immoral.
- Well-structured church discipline maximizes the opportunity for restoration and sets your church up to protect other churches if restoration is unsuccessful.

FOLLOW UP RESOURCES

- Document and Video: "Restorative Church Discipline Process (Structured Guide & Video)" by Brad Hambrick; http://brad-hambrick.com/churchdiscipline/

- Article: "Why We Should Always Teach Romans 13 with Romans 12" by Brad Hambrick; http://bradhambrick.com/romans13/

- Article: "Pastoral Wisdom and the Mandate to Report Abuse" by Julie Lowe; https://www.ccef.org/pastoral-wisdom-and-mandate -report-abuse/

- Article: "How Pastors Can Best Help Victims of Domestic Abuse" by Justin Holcomb; http://justinholcomb.com/2015/07/18/how -pastors-can-best-help-victims-of-domestic-abuse/

Ministry Responsibilities: Abuse Against a Minor vs. Abuse Against an Adult

There are important legal distinctions about what should happen (1) when there is abuse or neglect toward a child, elderly, or disabled person as compared to (2) when abuse occurs toward an able-bodied adult. In this lesson we will focus on children, but the same principles apply for individuals who lack the full capability to care for themselves.

If a pastor is going to honor Romans 13, then that pastor must understand these differences. Efforts to protect and ensure safety are *our Christian duty* regardless of the age of the person being oppressed; however *our civil obligations* do change based upon the age or capacity of the victim.

Reporting abuse is *mandated* when it is against a minor. Children have neither the level of independence to seek safety nor the intellectual capacity to understand what is happening in abuse, so our governing authorities have said they will intervene on a child's behalf. For example, the relevant North Caroline statute reads:

> "Any person or institution who has cause to suspect that a child under age 18 is abused, neglected, or dependent must make a report to the county department of social services (G.S. 7B-301).

As long as the reporter is acting in good faith, they cannot be held liable (G.S. 7B-309)."

Most state laws are very similar. Appendix A of this handbook includes all fifty state laws regarding: (a) mandated reporting laws for abuse in each state and relevant pastor-parishioner privilege, (b) the statute of limitations for criminal prosecution of sexual assault or past abuse, and (c) age requirements pertaining to statutory rape and sex between minors.

Every church should review these statutes with an attorney in their state for the most recent version of these laws. Ask the attorney to translate the laws into common language for you and ask questions until you understand the implications of each statute for your state.

MINISTRY REFLECTION

When have you been hesitant to act because you didn't know the legal requirement to report, limits on pastor-parishioner privilege, or another relevant legal issue? Use the resource in Appendix A to make sure you and your fellow staff members are not in this position again.

_____

_____

_____

_____

_____

As we think about abuse against a minor, there are three contexts we will consider:

1. a child disclosing an experience of abuse
2. observations of a child that make us "reasonably suspicious" abuse may be occurring,
3. hearing from a parent or other adult who knows about the abuse, and is confused about what to do next

Disclosure from a Minor: When you realize a child may be disclosing an experience of abuse, you want to affirm their choice to speak. For children, the unpleasant feelings that often come with talking about bad experiences can easily be mistaken for guilt.

You want to let the minor know, "I may not be able to keep everything you tell me confidential. If you are in danger, I have a responsibility to make sure you are safe. That may require us to involve people who can help us make sure you're safe." This is not to dissuade their disclosure, but help protect the child from feeling betrayed by the report that is filed.

HEAR FROM THE EXPERTS

 Question for Subject Area Experts: What are the best practices for making a child feel comfortable disclosing abuse without being leading or dismissive? When in the disclosure conversation should reporting be discussed? How much information should a ministry leader seek to obtain in an initial conversation? What is pastorally wise and what is better left to a counseling context?

 Answers from Subject Area Experts: Watch the experts' responses at churchcares.com, under the Video Training section, in the video entitled: *Lesson 3 – Ministry Responsibilities: Abuse Against a Minor vs. Abuse Against an Adult.*

Karla Siu: The main thing to understand when talking with a child is where they are developmentally. We need to speak to children in a "language and logic that **they** understand," as a good friend of mine always says, "Talking to a two-year-old about abuse is different than talking to a teenager about abuse." Both in terms of how they experience and interpret abuse and in terms of how you ask them about abuse and how they are able to communicate about the abuse.

The main goal at this juncture is to provide safety and security, both in word and action. We provide safety by listening, and we *do not* prod further, as this is outside the role of pastoral or lay ministry training and expertise and has negative implications both legally and psychologically for that child. You should simply listen to what the child voluntarily shares. It is okay to reassure the child in a developmentally appropriate manner that you heard what they had to say. Paraphrasing or repeating their exact words without too much affect and reaction is a good approach. Overreacting will invariably shut children down, and has a host of other undesired impacts on the victim. Remaining neutral but empathic creates safety in your relationship, and communicates that you are able to hold the delicate information they are entrusting you with thoughtfully.

You must also find a clear yet sensitive way to let the child know that you'll be making a report. It is best practice to share early on in the conversation because you want to build trust, and you also need to communicate that what has happened to them is not okay. Children are often scared of the implications of disclosing, particularly if the abuser is someone that they depend on for food, shelter, or have other emotional ties to the abuser (such as a popular youth pastor), so it's critical that you understand the possible implications and outcomes of the disclosure for that child and work to protect them as best you can through this process. Communicate the steps you will take but do not make promises you cannot keep. You can reassure them with your willingness to walk through this scary and difficult thing together. It's important to not provide false hope, but it is important to communicate care and reassurance of your support for them.

Andrea Munford: When a child discloses abuse, it's important to ensure their safety. Let them know that they are safe, and that you will be calling people whose job it is to help them. It's crucial that a child does not feel pressured to say what they think an adult is expecting them to say, therefore it's better not to ask the child specific questions. What often occurs is that an adult not trained in the correct manner asks a child direct questions that leads a child in their response. It also creates a need for a child to tell what happened to them again to investigators and social workers. Best practice is for the child to be interviewed by someone certified in Forensic Interviewing. This process also brings together a multi-disciplinary team (MDT) committed to providing a safe environment and necessary resources for a child and their family, as well as ensuring the integrity of a potential criminal investigation. This MDT approach is also important so a child does not have to repeat their story multiple times.

At the very onset of a disclosure of child abuse—whether physical, sexual, or even emotional—or of neglect, law enforcement should be notified immediately to determine the next steps. Child Protective Services should also be called when the offender is a parent or caregiver; however, if there is any question as to whether the offender has regular access to the child, it's better to just call CPS. These calls should be made outside the presence of the child, but be mindful not to the leave the child alone while placing calls, or to leave them with someone they may not be familiar with, as this could leave them feeling unsafe. Also be mindful not to leave a child alone with an offending parent or other person that could have an interest in protecting the offender, as they may harm the child or attempt to silence the child about the abuse.

Observable Marks of Abuse: You may see a child with bruises, scars, broken bones, or a flinch reflex to movements from a nearby adult. You may notice highly sexualized or aggressive behavior in a child too young to understand the significance of their actions. You may notice artwork or writing with themes that reveal an awareness of abusive behaviors and pain that are beyond what is age appropriate.

We will discuss in later lessons the best care responses to physical and sexual abuse. In this lesson, what you need to know is that these traits represent the legal standard for "reasonable suspicion" for which a report should be made. It is not the role of the church to investigate these matters, but to ensure that they are investigated by civil authorities and to care for the child.

HEAR FROM THE EXPERTS

(Q) **Question for Subject Area Experts:** What are the best practices for weighing the significance of observable marks of potential abuse and how does a ministry leader discern whether these things reach the threshold of "reasonable suspicion"?

(A) **Answers from Subject Area Experts:** Watch the experts' responses at churchcares.com, under the Video Training section, in the video entitled: *Lesson 3 – Ministry Responsibilities: Abuse Against a Minor vs. Abuse Against an Adult.*

Darby Strickland: The law requires that you make a report as soon as you have REASONABLE SUSPICION. We use the word *reasonable* all the time but the term "reasonable" can seem confusing in this context. This confusion is completely understandable and compounded by two competing pressures. The first is our own fear of what might happen if I make a report that turns out to be unfounded, and the second is our strong desire to protect a child or vulnerable person.

It helps to keep in mind it is not your responsibility to know or prove that a child has been abused. A report is not an accusation, but rather a request to investigate a situation. It can be easy to convince ourselves that since we know the people involved that we will be more careful and pastoral in our evaluation. But not only is it illegal to fail to report suspected abuse, this way of thinking fails to recognize that we do not have the special training it takes to investigate and interview potential victims—we are not equipped to uncover the truth or to recognize *predatory behavior*. This is why we do not have to be sure that something has occurred; we just have to be observing things that lead us to believe that abuse is one possible explanation for what we are seeing or hearing.

So when bruises, welts, burns, fractures, lacerations are unexplained or the explanation you are provided with does not ring true—it is reasonable to suspect that a child is being harmed. When a child is frightened of their parents, afraid to go home, *displays early sexualization* or reports injury, or sex abuse by their parents or any another person, you have cause to suspect or believe that child abuse is occurring. Any suspected form of sexual abuse whether physical contact, electronic, image based or exploitative must be reported. Reasonable suspicion means that you have seen physical or behavioral signs of maltreatment or that you have received a disclosure from a child about abuse or neglect. Remember, it is not your job to discern if the disclosures are true, you simply must report them.

Samantha Kilpatrick: In most states, Child Protective Services is set up to take reports of abuse and neglect by a parent or caretaker. When a call comes in to the local agency a screener evaluates and determines if the circumstances warrant investigation. The laws are clear as to the types of cases the agency has the authority to investigate. Cases that do not meet the criteria are not pursued by the agency, and CPS will often inform callers to call the local police if they feel that a crime is occurring.

State laws address who must report, what must be reported, the timing of a report, and the knowledge required by the reporter. Questions seem to arise around the knowledge required to make a report. My advice is always to err on the side of reporting. The language regarding knowledge varies among states—"cause to suspect," "reasonable suspicion," "reasonable belief," "reasonable cause to suspect," or "knows or has reason to suspect." Clearly if you have direct knowledge and proof, there is not a question—report; however, that is usually not the case. The standard in most states requires more than a feeling, but far less than certainty. So you must take the details that you know and make a determination based on your state's standard. Again, when in doubt, err on the side of making a report. The law does not require reporters to have first-hand knowledge of abuse nor does it encourage reporters to verify or investigate.

Again, here is where connections to these agencies should happen before a crisis. Consult with an attorney or Child Protective Services to become informed about your state's requirements for what to report, how to report, and timing of reporting. In all states, there are mandated reporters of abuse—some designate all adults as mandated reporters while others set out a list of mandated reporters. No matter what your state's law, even if you are not a mandated reporter, you are a permitted reporter—meaning you can always report. When you make a report, document your conversation with the CPS intake person. In addition, if it is physical or sexual abuse—this is criminal and the police should be contacted.

Talking to a Parent or Other Adult: Chances are, the parent talking to you also knows the powerlessness of being abused. They're not just sharing their child's story; they are likely sharing their own.

It is important to share your obligation to report; even if the adult or parent is the abuser.

But in addition to that: listen to their questions, help them organize their questions, *invite them to make the phone call to Child Protective Services with you,* ensure them you'll make sure they get guidance on their questions before the CPS conversation concludes, make sure the social worker explains what next steps will be taken, discuss with the social worker what safety precautions are advisable, take notes to help your friend remember what is being said, and listen to your friend as they process their fears as the conversation concludes.

Your job—in addition to making sure the report is made—is twofold: (a) make sure your friend faces no preventable surprises, and (b) ensure your friend knows that he or she does not have to remember everything that is being said.

This brings us to the second half of our subject: *what is different when abuse is only against an adult* (meaning no minors are involved *or* exposed)? What if this spouse we were just speaking about came and told us the same story but no children were in the home?

When abuse is against an adult, the adult victim is granted the choice about whether to get a restraining order (civil court) or pressing charges (criminal court). This is a legitimately difficult decision. Legal action makes their experience public and requires them to go through a legal process where "innocent until proven guilty" requires cross examination. Allowing the victim to make this decision is part of restoring their voice and giving them back a sense of control over the major events of their life. *It is wise for a victim to make this decision with the advisement of a counselor and/or attorney experienced with abuse cases and the legal process.*

MINISTRY REFLECTION

Place yourself in the position of someone who has been beaten or raped. You want justice and protection. You also want privacy and to live as if these things never happened. You can't have both. What would taking legal action cost you? What would remaining silent cost you? How would you weigh through this decision? What factors would impact your choice?

Note: Be careful not to read what you *would* do onto what a victim *should* do.

_____

_____

_____

_____

_____

A common mistake regarding abuse is premature intervention with the abuser. Until the victim has a plan and is emotionally ready to withstand reaction of the abuser, no confrontation should occur. Developing a safety plan is the first step in ministry for an adult victim of abuse. The most dangerous time for a victim of abuse is when they are considering separation for safety and the time period just after they leave.

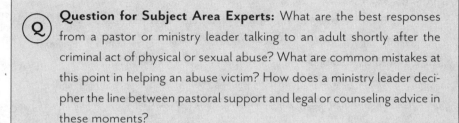

HEAR FROM THE EXPERTS

Q **Question for Subject Area Experts:** What are the best responses from a pastor or ministry leader talking to an adult shortly after the criminal act of physical or sexual abuse? What are common mistakes at this point in helping an abuse victim? How does a ministry leader decipher the line between pastoral support and legal or counseling advice in these moments?

A **Answers from Subject Area Experts:** Watch the experts' responses at churchcares.com, under the Video Training section, in the video entitled: *Lesson 3 – Ministry Responsibilities: Abuse Against a Minor vs. Abuse Against an Adult.*

Leslie Vernick: When someone you know and care about is violated, you want to do something. You want to protect them, to fix it, you want to make their pain go away.

If you can understand this important truth, you will be huge help. The truth is: THERE IS NOTHING you can do in this moment that will take their pain away or make their problem instantly better. So the pressure is off.

But what you can do is respectfully and carefully listen. Validate that you are glad they told you.

What you want to create in this initial disclosure is a safe space where the victim feels heard, believed, safe, and cared for. Like Job's friends did when they initially sat silently with Job in his pain, you can do that more powerfully with your presence than with your words.

But in our anxiety we sometimes make costly mistakes that actually do harm to the victim.

First, asking for details or trying to verify the victim's story to make sure it's truthful is not your place. There will be time for that if and when a police report is made. You are not the investigator. You are the pastor or a ministry leader. The shepherd who is to comfort and protect the sheep who's just got bit and abused by a wolf.

In a victim's trauma, memory details can become fuzzy. Don't be surprised if the abused person sounds contradictory, confused, or even furious and uses salty language to express strong emotions.

Second. This is not the time to help a victim reframe this experience, or to look for what God is doing or to help find the silver lining. There will be those opportunities much later in the counseling process but in the initial disclosure, simply be a comforting presence, show great respect for the victims feelings and boundaries.

When someone has been violated, their "no" was disrespected. That's the last thing you want to repeat right now. If the victim doesn't want to call the police or to talk about the details, honor that. Allow the victim a "no," even if you don't think it's the wisest choice. That shows a deep respect for the victim's God-given personhood and their freedom to choose, which after being violated, he or she needs to remember and reclaim.

Last, sometimes our questions can sound like blaming the victim for being victimized. For example: "What did you do to provoke her?" OR, "Why didn't you tell someone sooner?"

These may be legitimate questions for the victim to ponder much later in counseling, but when they are asked prematurely they heap blame and shame upon the victim and you will not feel like a safe person.

Your job right now is listen, give support, and help the victim find the next step resources that will bring healing, justice, and closure.

Samantha Kilpatrick: The only and best response to an adult who is disclosing physical or sexual abuse is to listen with compassion, validate the story, and offer support. Look for ways to help the person feel more comfortable—ask if there is someone he or she would like present, maybe a friend who can provide some additional support. Out of your sincere desire to help, your first inclination may be to try to make things better or solve the problem. And out of that desire to help, a common mistake is for you as the authority figure to start making decisions for the person in front of you. Remember that the dynamic of abuse is about power and control and by stepping in to solve and make decisions, you are taking control rather than helping the person in front of you regain some control.

One of your first concerns must be safety—what happens when this person leaves your office. In advance, you and your staff should understand basic safety planning or know someone who can immediately help. If what is disclosed sounds criminal in nature, you need to encourage and help the individual make contact with law enforcement or a lawyer who works with victims of abuse. Offer to go with them or suggest a support person who will go with them.

Another common and potentially lethal mistake is a church leader who decides to take matters into his own hands and investigate or confront the abuser. This is unwise and dangerous in so many ways—it puts the victim in great danger and may negatively impact a criminal investigation.

KEY POINTS OF THIS LESSON

- Reporting abuse is mandated when there is "reasonable suspicion" of abuse against a minor.
- Every church should discuss their state specific laws regarding abuse with an attorney.
- Premature confrontation of the abuser by church leaders can make the victim(s) less safe.
- The decision about whether to take legal action by an adult abuse victim is a difficult one that should be made with advisement from a counselor and/or attorney experienced with abuse cases.

FOLLOW UP RESOURCES

- Article: "Overcoming Codependency" by Brad Hambrick; http://bradhambrick.com/codependencypc/

- Book: *The Emotionally Destructive Marriage* by Leslie Vernick

- Article: "How to Develop a Safety Plan for Domestic Violence" by Brad Hambrick; http://bradhambrick.com/safetyplan/

- Article: "When Is Reporting Abuse Mandated?" by Diane Langberg; http://www.dianelangberg.com/2018/07/twitter-question-mandated-reporting/

- Article: "Reporting Child Sexual Abuse: FAQ's" by Darkness to Light; www.d2l.org/wp-content/uploads/2017/01/Reporting_Child_Sexual_Abuse-Small-File.pdf

- Article: "What Is Child Abuse and Neglect? Recognizing the Signs and Symptoms" by Child Welfare; https://www.childwelfare.gov/pubPDFs/whatiscan.pdf#page=5&view=Recognizing%20Signs%20of%20Abuse%20and%20Neglec

- Hotline: The Childhelp National Child Abuse Hotline is available by phone 24/7 at 1-800-4-A-CHILD (1-800-422-4453). Childhelp is also not a reporting agency, but if you have questions about what is considered child abuse in your state, or what would happen if you made a Child Protective Services (CPS) report or went to the police about your concerns, they can answer them.

Ministry Partners: Awareness of Key Professionals in Victim Advocate Roles

The relationship between ministry leaders and social workers or mental health professionals has not always been a good one. At one level, this is surprising because both have devoted their vocations to helping people in the midst of their greatest emotional-relational-spiritual brokenness. At another level, it is not surprising because of differences that emerge between these two professions.

Social workers and mental health professionals *are beholden to one individual or family at a time*. They have a series of isolated helping relationships, and each choice they make is for the flourishing of that individual.

By contrast, pastors *are beholden to an entire congregation and care for each individual as a member of the group*. Each choice a pastor makes has the felt sense of being a precedent for the entire congregation.

When providing care in an abuse context—which is always interpersonal and is usually marked by wildly varying renditions of what actually happened—these differences have immense implications.

MINISTRY REFLECTION

When a pastor offers advice for one situation, this usually has far-reaching consequences. For example, when a pastor gives marriage/relationship advice, this often gets circulated as his counsel for all marriages/relationships. With this in mind, how do you think a pastor's sense of obligation to an entire congregation impacts the counsel he gives? When and how would this be an advantage? On the other hand, how does it limit the willingness of ministry leaders to acknowledge some of the unique challenges that exist in an abusive relationship? What advice do you typically give married couples that would not be right to give to a couple dealing with abuse?

_____

_____

_____

_____

_____

Too often the tension that exists between the advisements of pastors and social workers is exclusively chalked up to what they believe about the Bible, marriage, or morality. While theological differences often do exist, a good working relationship between ministry leaders and social workers is possible and necessary.

To help you navigate these waters, we want you to be able to do two things once this lesson is finished:

1. Name, define, and describe the roles of three key professionals in victim advocate roles.
2. Provide an overview of key ethical limitations for these individuals.

First, **Child Protection Services**, or CPS for short. CPS is a locally run government organization tasked with protecting children. CPS is sometimes called the Department of Children and Families. CPS workers are often called social workers; we will talk about them next. However, not everyone who works for CPS is a social worker and not all social workers work for CPS.

Here are three ethical limitations for CPS that ministry leaders need to be aware of:

1. CPS *adheres to strict confidentiality policies.* This can sometimes create a sense of frustration and mistrust from ministry leaders. CPS depends on the family to communicate for themselves with those offering assistance unless you have been identified as a caretaker for the children.

2. CPS *prioritizes the vulnerability of victims in their approach to interviewing.* For instance, when it is reported that a father has abused his child, CPS will first attempt to see the child and assure their safety before interviewing the mother, and then lastly, the perpetrator of abuse. *Alerting a suspected perpetrator that CPS has been or will be contacted alters the course of a CPS investigation and can put a victim at risk.*

3. CPS *has an ethical and legal obligation to consider the parents' wishes for their children,* including which of their friends and neighbors can be considered for temporary placement. As long as the parents' wishes do not put the children in immediate risk of harm, CPS must prioritize the parents' wishes.

KEY TIPS WHEN WORKING WITH CPS

- Provide as much information as you know.

- Present as many resources from your ministry as possible (i.e., offering short-term residence for spouse, or providing a foster family for children) to help the family.
- Offer to be present for meetings with CPS and attend court dates. In those settings, confidentiality is expanded to those present but *you can only come to these meetings at the parents' request.*

HEAR FROM THE EXPERTS

Q **Question for Subject Area Experts:** How can a ministry leader proactively (before a crisis) develop a good working relationship with CPS? What are common pitfalls that harm the working relationship with CPS—topics a ministry leader could discuss in their pro-active relationship building with CPS?

A **Answers from Subject Area Experts:** Watch the experts' responses at churchcares.com, under the Video Training section, in the video entitled: *Lesson 4 – Ministry Partners: Awareness of Key Professionals in Victim Advocate Roles.*

Mika Edmondson: The thought of Child Protective Services doesn't engender warm feelings in the minds of many pastors. That is most likely because we don't hear the stories of the thousands of cases they handle well, we usually only hear about few problematic cases. I'd like to suggest that when approached correctly CPS can be a valuable resource in helping churches advocate for the most vulnerable among us, our children who are often unable to advocate for themselves.

It's vital that congregations begin proactively equipping themselves as soon as possible, before abuse occurs so that they will be in a better position to respond in wisdom and love. For these reasons, it's important pastors to suspend negative preconceptions about CPS and begin to view it as a valuable resource and develop a good rapport with local CPS workers. Pastors can begin by visiting and reading through the CPS website for their local state or municipality. Secondly they can call and speak with a CPS worker, clearly stating their intentions to learn from CPS and use it as an ongoing resource for abuse prevention as well as response. Finally, if possible, congregations may avail themselves of pertinent trainings and information that CPS has to offer.

Let's talk about what ministry leaders could learn from CPS workers. First, CPS workers are trained to recognize the subtle signs of abuse and neglect invisible to the untrained eye and so they are extremely helpful at equipping the congregation in how to spot abuse.

Second, they also have a mandate to advocate particularly for the safety and well-being of children. As pastors think of the varied interests of all family members and adults involved in an allegation of child abuse, it's easy to de-center the interest of affected children. Adults are much better able to advocate for their interests than children, and so it's helpful for pastors to regularly consult with experts who focus their full attention on the needs of children. Most CPS workers also have valuable experience and insight into local policies and laws on abuse. They can help pastors and congregations develop a basic familiarity not only with the various forms of abuse, but also with local policies and laws around child abuse as well as local resources for children in distress. Since clergy persons and even church volunteers like nursery workers are often considered mandated reporters, CPS can also equip congregations to understand how to recognize and carry out that responsibility as well.

Karla Siu: The best way for us to relate to each other is to enter into relationship with one another. I cannot relate to you unless I actually interact with you. It's human nature to have preconceived notions. It follows, then, that we aren't the only ones making assumptions about CPS workers. CPS workers are **also** making assumptions about pastors and ministers!

This is why we encourage you to reach out to your local CPS, and to start the conversation with the understanding that the main role of Child Protective Services is to **investigate** an allegation of child abuse, and their primary goal is to **protect the child from harm to prevent re-injury**.

Here are two simple yet important tips that will facilitate your interactions with CPS workers:

1. Expect that CPS workers **cannot share information freely** with you. This is not because they don't want to; it's simply because they must adhere to strict confidentiality laws. By understanding this, it will allow both parties to talk about the case without feeling like CPS is withholding information and resisting cooperation.

2. Be factual! Do your best to gather as much verifiable information as possible **before** you pick up the phone to call CPS. I'm embarrassed to admit, that the first time I called CPS, I didn't have my client's address, phone number, and I didn't know the guardian's full name. If you put yourself in their shoes, there's really not much they can do with vague information. So be good listeners, take good notes, and be prepared to relay this information to them when you call.

To summarize, if you go into the conversation with a shared understanding about roles and goals, as well as the limits of confidentiality laws, **and** you are able to relay helpful information, you will lay a strong foundation for good relationships with your local CPS workers.

Second, let's discuss **social workers**. Social workers are professionals who have devoted themselves to enhancing the well-being of the vulnerable, oppressed, and those living in poverty. They may work in hospitals, doctor's offices, mental health clinics, schools, hospice, CPS, domestic violence clinics, shelters, or other non-profit organizations. Licensed clinical social workers (LCSW) can work as therapists and are sanctioned to diagnose mental health disorders and provide therapy.

Social workers are especially helpful in abusive situations for a variety of reasons: (1) their training on the impact of abuse, (2) their experience assessing abusive situations, and (3) their experience recognizing individual and family needs.

Here are three ethical limitations for social workers that ministry leaders need to be aware of:

1. Social workers are *always mandated reporters*. But this is the same standard ministry leaders are under, so this should not be a point of conflict.
2. Social workers *have to accept all religions and walks of life within their professional role*. They should support their client's (your church member's) religious goals. However, this means that a social worker cannot change their assessment of the case simply for immoral behavior. For instance, if an abusive spouse is also having an affair, this is not an "additional demerit" in the eyes of the social worker.
3. Social workers are also *under strict confidentiality guidelines similar to a CPS worker*. However, a church member can sign an information release for a church leader to speak with the social worker about cooperative care between therapy and the church.

KEY TIPS WHEN WORKING WITH SOCIAL WORKERS

- Ask that the abused church member under the care of a social worker request a release of information.
- Ask the social worker to provide their perspective on the key safety variables in play, how you or the church can best be a stabilizing force, and what effects of abuse that you might be

mislabeling in moral terms (for example, a trigger response to trauma sometimes comes off to church leaders as poor self-control in conflict).

HEAR FROM THE EXPERTS

 Question for Subject Area Experts: What are the best ways you've seen ministry leaders and social workers navigate the spiritual and moral neutrality within which a social worker has to operate? What are examples of the kind of helpful assessments a social worker can make in abuse cases?

 Answers from Subject Area Experts: Watch the experts' responses at churchcares.com, under the Video Training section, in the video entitled: *Lesson 4 – Ministry Partners: Awareness of Key Professionals in Victim Advocate Roles.*

Leslie Vernick: When you already have a working relationship with someone, it helps dispel some misconceptions about their role and facilitates more trust when you are thrown together to work through a crisis.

Social workers are not blank slates. They may have values that differ than Christian values or they may share some of the beliefs we have.

The difference, however, is that when they function professionally, they are trained to be aware of their own personal biases and try hard not to allow those beliefs or biases or even personal CORE values to influence their investigation or their recommendations—either in a positive or in a negative way.

For example, if a social worker was an atheist, or didn't believe in corporal punishment for disciplinary purposes, the social worker's personal biases or beliefs should not influence the outcome of his or her evaluation of a Christian family who was being investigated for child abuse.

The social worker might personally and professionally disapprove of corporal punishment, but as long as the parent did not legally meet the definition of abuse when spanking his or her child, the social worker's personal values are a non-issue.

Social workers are trained to assess abuse situations from a values neutral stance in order to make the best recommendations possible as well as elicit the facts around the situation in such a way to make the evidence they find hold up to legal scrutiny if such a path is necessary.

Social workers are also trained to take into account not only the individual's psychosocial history and mental health diagnosis, but also a person's ethnic, cultural, familial, and contextual history that may influence how the situation is viewed.

For example, in certain cultures or ethnic communities, spousal abuse may be more common and accepted, thus making it more difficult to convince an abused spouse to create a safety plan or separate from her abuser. This reality may impact minor children and their vulnerability living in such a household, which the social worker will have to factor into the recommendations made.

Most social workers do the work they do because they deeply care about the safety and well-being of children and other victims of abuse. They don't do it for the money nor for the perks as they pay is low and the work is hard, heartbreaking, and sometimes dangerous.

Social workers who are also clinically trained can be a huge asset in helping church leaders navigate through the necessary treatment options for genuine healing for the victim and perpetrator of abuse.

Most church leaders have not been trained in assessing mental health problems or trauma and its impact to the body, mind, and spirit of victims. Nor have they had adequate training in working with manipulative and abusive individuals.

Romans 13 reminds us that God has given us legal authorities to protect people and help them get safe and stay safe against evildoers. Church discipline and structure is important, but it has no legal jurisdiction to protect a child or keep a person safe.

For example, if a person accused of child sexual abuse chooses to leave the church, discontinue pastoral counseling, convinces his wife that he's changed, and decides to move back home with his minor children, the church has no legal authority to step in to protect or remove those children from his influence or care, but the law does.

Having open communication with trusted professionals and working together through the signed release of information helps you as the pastor, work in concert with other wise, helping professionals to bring the best possible outcome for healing to the individual and/or family involved.

Chris Moles: Neutrality can be difficult to navigate but it does not require an abandonment of one's faith or voice regarding what is true. When I first became involved in the work, there was some concern because I was a pastor. A lengthy discussion unfolded about what restrictions may need to be articulated to me about evangelism and the Bible, etc. One colleague challenged the group to view my faith position as a benefit to our work rather than a hindrance. That conversation lead to honest dialogue about the significance of my faith to the work. Since then I have served on a variety of teams, boards, and government programs all the while maintaining a commitment to my faith, and by the grace of God (and some kind people) freely offer Scripture, biblical principles, and faith-based advocacy for peace and safety.

I am not suggesting that social workers, or any people helpers intentionally violate policy, but I am suggesting that your faith should motivate you, and must inform your work. Now, with that said, we have the privilege of being an ally to Christian people helpers in a variety of settings by discussing matters of faith, praying with families, people helpers, judges, and court officials as well as offering counsel, comfort, and care to families. Here are three ways pastors can serve people helpers well:

1. Remain humble: We are leaders and with that can become accustomed to offering quick resolutions by "taking the bull by the horns" as it were. But, not only does the system not recognize us as an authority the complexities of these cases take time and energy that require us to slow down and look for places to lead through serving and partnering.

2. Demonstrate a teachable spirit: I often tell folks that I am training that it is tremendously helpful to come into difficult cases with the mentality that "I am the most ignorant person in the room." By that I mean that the folks directly involved know more than I do about their situation, the case workers involved know more about the system than I do, and the Holy Spirit knows more than all us. Asking good questions, listening to others, and learning on the job does more to prepare us than perhaps anything else.

3. Promote peace: After all, we're called to peace. We serve the Prince of Peace, and we're working together to introduce a kingdom of peace in a world of conflict.

Third, let's define and examine the role of a **Guardian ad-litem (GAL)**. A GAL is a trained community volunteer. Their role is to get to know the child, the child's living environment, their social environment, and what *the child's preferred outcomes* are in the pertinent decisions being made about their life.

GAL's are relevant in legal proceedings where it would be easy for the child's voice to be under-represented or manipulated. *If you are ministering to an abuse victim or someone being divorced who believes their child's interest is not getting adequate consideration, they can request that the judge assign a GAL.*

A GAL makes a recommendation to the court. Judges are not obligated to follow the GAL's reçommendations, but they do take them seriously.

Here are two ethical limitations for GAL's that ministry leaders need to be aware of.

1. GAL's are *only in an advisory role to the court and CPS.* They do *not* make recommendations to family members, children, pastors, etc.
2. GAL's are not capable of respecting the family's privacy because they have been tasked with gathering information as a means to supply the court with their recommendations.

HEAR FROM THE EXPERTS

 Question for Subject Area Experts: What are key do's and don'ts that a ministry leader could advise a parent concerning how to best relate to a GAL?

 Answers from Subject Area Experts: Watch the experts' responses at churchcares.com, under the Video Training section, in the video entitled: *Lesson 4 – Ministry Partners: Awareness of Key Professionals in Victim Advocate Roles.*

Karla Siu: When ministering to parents who are undergoing a custody litigation, it's very likely that the court has or will assign the child or the children a Guardian Ad Litem, or GAL, as they are more commonly referred to. The main things to know about GAL's is that their primary function is more that of an advocate than what we may typically understand as a "guardian." Put differently, the GAL at no point assumes official guardianship of the child he/she advocates for in court.

The other important thing to understand about GALs is that they are often community volunteers who may have varying levels of training and have diverse professional backgrounds. GALs advocate and give voice to the perspective of the child. They submit information to the court for consideration in the case, and form part of a multidisciplinary team of professionals including (but not limited to) attorneys, therapists/counselors, CPS social workers, etc.

As pastors and ministry leaders, it'll be important to maintain and promote healthy communication between the multidisciplinary teams and the families we are ministering to who are involved with the court system. Early on in the process you'll want to clarify your relationship with the multidisciplinary team and agree on communication and roles. In doing so, you will give yourself the ability to reference your mutual agreements when, and if, things get complicated. You'll also want to let the individual or family you are ministering to know that 1) you are open to working collaboratively with the multidisciplinary care team in place in order to help them and their family. 2) You will not act as a messenger between the family and any member of the team. Explain that you'll encourage them to speak directly with the appropriate team member, and that you will support them with this, but you won't be speaking on their behalf.

That said, reassure and remind parents that you are not there to take sides or to judge. You should feel free to remind them of your support as often as is needed. Stress the importance of making room for the process and teach them to ask questions to the appropriate care team member, to be assertive in communicating their needs. It would be appropriate in a support role to coach them through how they may be more effective communicators.

Parents should raise any concerns about a GAL with **their** own therapist and/or attorney. Therapists and lawyers have an ethical and professional responsibility to represent the **sole** interests of their clients, and as such become the natural advocate for a parent.

This approach allows each team member to fulfill their roles well and requires that we trust the systems in place to bring about the desired justice and care for the individual we are helping. So I invite you to see GALs as a resource, and to learn to lean on their role to do what they are tasked with doing—**advocate for our children by making their voices and needs heard.**

When CPS, social workers, or GALs are involved in a family's care, it means that danger has been involved and conflict is high. However, *their voice in the judicial process can bring stability to a situation that might be difficult to maintain with the mere peer influence of ministry leaders.*

MINISTRY REFLECTION

Imagine ministering to a family where there is volatile conflict. Imagine trying to adjudicate basic decency of interaction when one spouse gets aggressive with you (verbally or physically) as a minister. How easy is it, because you have no authority, to become as much a part of the problem as the solution? How does having someone with more jurisdictional authority help stabilize the situation to a degree that allows for the better ministry outcomes?

_____

_____

_____

_____

_____

KEY POINTS OF THIS LESSON

- Social workers are beholden to individuals. Pastors are beholden to a congregation. This allegiance-difference can create unnecessary conflict unless it is understood.
- It is important for ministry leaders to know the title, roles, and ethical restrictions of key victim advocates that can be beneficial in caring for abuse victims.
- The legal knowledge, authority, and jurisdiction of social workers can bring needed stability and accountability into abusive situations which are characteristically volatile. This should be viewed as a good and helpful thing.

FOLLOW UP RESOURCES

- Article: "Comparing Pastoral Ethics and Counseling Ethics" by Brad Hambrick; http://bradhambrick.com/comparing-pastoral-ethics-and-counseling-ethics/

- Article: "5 Types of Mental Health Professionals: Title, Education, and Purpose" by Brad Hambrick; http://bradhambrick.com/5-types-of-mental-health-professionals-title-education-and-purpose/

PART TWO

Key Responses *from* Pastors and Ministry Leaders

Key Responses to Sexual Abuse

The first and most important thing you need to realize when someone discloses the experience of sexual abuse is that they are demonstrating *an immense amount of courage.*

Maybe one of the least understood aspects of sexual abuse is the victim's loss of voice. Abuse is usually followed by demands not to tell anyone and threats of what will happen if the victim does talk. Then, once a victim is alone, their own sense of shame makes them not want to tell anyone. Finally, there are the fears of what they will have to endure if they tell someone and are believed, not to mention the fears of telling someone and not being believed.

By the time victims get to the point of talking to you as a ministry leader about their experience of sexual abuse, they are in the midst of navigating all of these fears. That is courage!

MINISTRY REFLECTION

Reflect on the journey a sexual abuse victim has taken to get to a conversation with you: the assault(s), threats, or minimizing language from their abuser, personal shame, fear, sorting out lies from truth, wondering if it was their fault, uncertainty of what will happen if they disclose their experience. When someone speaks to you about sexual abuse, realize that what is a "first conversation" for you is "a long way down a weary journey" for them. Honor the moment as such.

_____

_____

_____

_____

_____

By the end of the initial conversation with a victim, you should help them make decisions about what legal steps need to be taken and what self-care steps are wise. *But if we fixate on the end of the conversation, we will turn delicate conversations of pastoral care into cold conversations of legal obligation.*

If a victim feels uncared for or unbelieved, they recoil and begin to think they've made a mistake in talking. Their statements begin to contradict one another and a moment of potential healing only reinforces pain. But this time, pain is multiplied by the fact that even their church (representing God) failed them.

You may be thinking, "This feels complicated and messy. It feels like more than I'm trained to do." It is messy. Welcome, again, to the life of someone who has been abused. It is not as complicated as it appears, but abuse (even hearing of someone else's abuse) does cloud our thinking. You may not be trained to walk the full journey of restoration with someone, but as a ministry leader, it is part of our gospel calling to at least walk the first steps of this journey well. That is what this lesson is intended to train you to do.

HEAR FROM THE EXPERTS

 Question for Subject Area Experts: What are good pastoral practices for receiving an initial disclosure of sexual abuse? What are common mistakes? How can ministry leaders know if they're doing a good job when nothing in the emotional atmosphere of the room will offer positive affirmations that things are being done well?

 Answers from Subject Area Experts: Watch the experts' responses at churchcares.com, under the Video Training section, in the video entitled: *Lesson 5 – Key Responses to Sexual Abuse.*

Diane Langberg: Keep in mind that when someone comes to see you to talk about abuse they are attempting to tell you something they most want to forget. They are afraid of what happened, of the person who did it, of you and your reactions, as well as of remembering and speaking out loud. They are afraid of what you will think of them. They feel overwhelmed. Keep your voice quiet and slow. Do not make sudden movements. If they look fine, that does not mean they are fine.

Your main task is to listen well. They will not tell an ordered story. Most abuse/rape stories come out fragmented and disordered. They may say things you want to correct. This is not the time for that. If they are reporting abuse by someone you know or work with, you will want to deny it, defend the accused, and may feel anxious about how this will affect others. You will need to put your own fears and questions aside for the moment. You are giving them a safe space to tell a frightening and often shame-ridden story at their pace. The purpose of listening is to honor the teller in a safe place so that you may begin to grasp in some measure what it is like to be them. Let them know that what they are doing is courageous and is the right thing to do. They are speaking truth and dragging darkness into the light. Abuse silences victims and renders them powerless. Listening makes room for their voice and restores dignity. And frankly, they have honored you by coming to you. You have been seen as safe—as a shepherd is meant to be—when they feel most vulnerable. Keep in mind that their vulnerability has already been exploited. Let them know you want them to be safe too and you want to help them get the care that they need.

Darby Strickland: Romans 12:9–12 tells us we are to bear one another's burdens, especially when someone is facing evil. We are called to be compassionate, gentle, and patient in our care. This is harder to do than it seems. Many sex abuse, victims have been conditioned by their abusers to feel responsible for the abuse and not to complain when another person is hurting them. Their voice has been devalued, threatened, or even squashed by someone in authority. So they tend not to speak up in the moment and let you know that what you are doing or saying is wounding them. In contrast, some victim's cries for help and complaints can be mistakenly reduced to unrighteous anger. We are called to see past a victim's presentation and bring our own awareness as to what is helpful and what is hurtful.

When a victim is disclosing sex abuse, I would encourage you to seek to protect their story. Do not ask too many questions about the details. Often times questions are experienced as disbelief or result in further guilt and shame. Ask broader questions, *How are you doing?*, *How can I help you?*, and *What are you fearful of?* Take a person's cue as to what they are comfortable sharing. You do not need details to imagine the horror of it all or to help. Also, be mindful of your role, this is especially important if you are a pastor or elder. What will it be like in the days ahead for them as they sit in church or take communion from you if you know the intimate details?

Do your best to stay present with them in the moment, listening to their heart, their wounds, and their concerns. There will be plenty of time later for you to contemplate which next steps you have to take and how this disclosure might affect you or your church. Avoid interjecting comments or questions that address your fears and concerns, like *Do you think our elders will believe you?* Stay focused on their story and their suffering.

Finally, be willing to sit in the mess with them, as Jesus would. There is nothing you can say in this moment to fix it. Instead look for ways to affirm both their courage in bringing evil into the light, and the depths of their suffering.

Rachael Denhollander: When you respond to a disclosure of abuse, two guiding principles can help inform your response:

First, know and remember the lies victims so often hear in their minds. Let your responses speak the truth to those lies and be very careful not to reflect them in any way.

Express grief, let them know you recognize the evil they have experienced, and it matters. "I am so sorry. This is wrong. I am grieved to know you have suffered this way. This grieves the heart of God."

Affirm they are not responsible and bear no shame or guilt. And emphasize that you believe them. Speak the truth about what they describe and use the right terms where appropriate—abuse, crime—help them correctly identify what they've told you.

Second, know and remember the damage that is done in abuse, so that your response stands in contrast to that damage. One of the most important things taken from a victim is their ability to choose, so ask questions designed to give the victim a voice and the ability to control the situation. Even simple questions, like whether they would like the door opened or closed, someone else in the room, or not, can help the survivor feel more secure.

Bear in mind the lies the victim likely believes, and the damage that has been done, and respond in a way that stands in contrast to it.

After focusing on care and honoring the courage of an initial disclosure of abuse, we should turn our attention to what ought to be done next, either by legal obligation or Christian duty. To discern this, consider again the concepts of Lesson 3: for abuse of minors, reporting is mandated and for abuse against adults, the victim chooses if legal steps are taken.

HEAR FROM THE EXPERTS

(Q) **Question for Subject Area Experts:** What are key skills and points of focus when a minor discloses the experience of sexual abuse for each of the three phases of this initial conversation: (1) being supportive during the disclosure, (2) communicating the need to make a report, and (3) comforting the minor about what will happen next? When is it wise or unwise to call CPS with the child present?

(A) **Answers from Subject Area Experts:** Watch the experts' responses at churchcares.com, under the Video Training section, in the video entitled: *Lesson 5 – Key Responses to Sexual Abuse.*

Samantha Kilpatrick: When an individual discloses sexual abuse, you, the church leader, must assume a place similar to that of Christ as Immanuel (God with us). This is not a time to teach, interrogate, or investigate. This is a time to listen, to validate, and to assess what needs to happen next.

In assessing what needs to happen next, think safety first—what needs to happen before this individual leaves. Your next thought should be about reporting—become familiar with the laws of your state and make community connections prior to a crisis. Pastors and ministry leaders, this is a difficult part of your job and you need not travel it alone. When faced with the decision about reporting abuse to the authorities, think about these four things. First, is this child abuse as defined by my state—keep an updated copy of the laws handy. Your state's law will define what constitutes child abuse, including acts and omissions and definitions of perpetrators. Remember you do not need to investigate or have direct proof; "reasonable suspicion" or "cause to suspect" is enough.

Second, know whether you are mandated reporter. In some states, all adults are mandated reporters, while in others a listed group of professionals are mandated reporters. In most states members of the clergy are mandated reporters. And third, know who you should call. Finally, if it does not meet the definition of child abuse in your state or you are not a mandated reporter, consider the safety of the child and others and whether you need to call the police and report a crime. Remember a child is at risk, and a delay or failure to report means that the child is still a target of abuse and is not safe. Err on the side of asking for guidance. Local social workers and police officers would be happy help you think through wise next steps to ensure safety.

Andrea Munford: Make sure the child feels safe and that they aren't being made to feel like they've done something wrong. Phrases such as, "Thank you for telling me what happened" can help make a child feel like that it's okay that they told someone.

The age of the child should determine how much information is shared directly with them. Choosing phrases that are age appropriate can be helpful, such as telling a very young child that you are going to call someone whose job is to help children, versus telling a fifteen-year-old that you need to call CPS and the police so they can investigate what happened.

Simple phrases such as, "I want to make sure you are safe so I'm going to call people who can help" will help children understand why you need to make those calls. Just be prepared to answer honestly if they ask who those people are because if you are evasive or untruthful they will feel further mistrust and doubtful that anyone cares about helping them.

Having made many CPS notifications in my career, there are questions you may need to answer that are not suitable for children to hear. If it's safe to do so, leave the child with a non-offending parent or with a trusted member of the church. If a child needs to remain near, advise the CPS case worker that the child is with you so they will understand your need to answer some questions being mindful of what the child may hear.

If you are talking with *an adult who has been abused as a child*, a question that needs to be raised during this initial conversation is, "Does your abuser have any access to children at this time?" If the answer is "yes," then this constitutes "reasonable suspicion" of a child being abused and a CPS report needs to be made.

However, there are instances of date rape, sexual assault, or sexual abuse in marriage where no children are known to be in harm's way. This does not mean that no legal actions should be taken; it just means that prompt reporting to an agency like CPS is not mandated.

In the case where no children are in harm's way, victims can put their own well-being in the forefront of their decision-making regarding legal action. The victim can ask questions like: *What would the emotional cost of going through of pressing charges? Am I ready for that? What would I need to do to be ready for that legal process? What are the emotional costs of not pressing charges? Am I okay with nothing being done?*

As a ministry leader, you don't have to be the primary one helping the victim weigh all of those questions. In an initial conversation, that would be overwhelming. Your role in this early stage is to (a) assure the victim that these are good questions to ask, (b) assure them of support in whatever answer they choose, and (c) help connect them with someone experienced in working with abuse victims.

MINISTRY REFLECTION

Think of a question you needed to ask, but felt guilty for considering. For example, maybe asking for time off during a season of burnout? What would it have meant for a trusted person in your life to (a) believe you were working hard and hurting, (b) affirm it was wise to take time off, and (c) connect you with someone who could help you think through how to recover? In the initial early stages when an abuse victim is considering their options that they feel guilty for asking about, this is the kind of role you play.

_____

_____

_____

_____

_____

This means you have at least one more role in that initial conversation; after (a) hearing the victim's story, (b) affirming their courage, and (c) validating their options, the last point of focus is this: (d) you need to help them find a good counselor. In any given community, the number and quality of options will vary. Your role is simply to help this individual to connect with the best of who is available in your community. In the follow up resource section of this lesson, we give you guidance on how to find quality counselors in your city and how to vet counselors that are a good fit for your members.

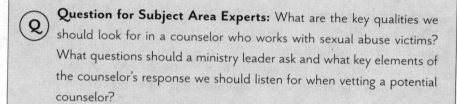

HEAR FROM THE EXPERTS

Q **Question for Subject Area Experts:** What are the key qualities we should look for in a counselor who works with sexual abuse victims? What questions should a ministry leader ask and what key elements of the counselor's response we should listen for when vetting a potential counselor?

A **Answers from Subject Area Experts:** Watch the experts' responses at churchcares.com, under the Video Training section, in the video entitled: *Lesson 5 – Key Responses to Sexual Abuse.*

Diane Langberg: A counselor who works with victims of sexual abuse needs to understand the impact that trauma has on a person. Victims live with the recurring, tormenting memories of atrocities witnessed and/or borne. It infects their sleep with horrific nightmares, destroys their relationships, their capacity to work or study, torments their emotions and shatters their faith and mutilates hope. Many are rendered mute, numb, and unmoving. Trauma is indeed extraordinary, not because it rarely happens but because it overwhelms normal human coping. Counselors who understand will work in a way that reverses the dynamics of the trauma. They will provide safety for the vulnerable; encourage them to give voice to both the abuse and its effects even though it takes a long time. Good counselors will also want to restore a sense of choice and dignity to the victim and will not be overbearing or demanding of a certain pace or response.

I encourage pastors to read a book or two about abuse so they have some understanding of it, as that will help them care for their own people as well as find them good counselors. I also recommend they meet with or at least speak by phone with a counselor asking them such questions as: *How long have you worked with abuse victims? Any idea about how many you have seen? What kind of training have you gotten for working with this population? What experts have influenced your approach to this area? Are you a licensed counselor (a state license usually requires training regarding mandated reporting and ethics)?* I have met with many pastors and some have apologized for their inquiries. I tell them a good shepherd will always want to confirm that when they make a recommendation that they have already checked it out. Please know that this work does not go quickly. You cannot damage anyone, and even more so a malleable child, and have that damage erased by a few words. Working with the traumatized is a ministry of restraint, of slowing down and of little by little. It is a small taste of our Almighty God becoming flesh on our behalf. He became like us so that we might become like Him. It is the ministry of small things, of going back for lost things. I have found the work to be what I call a front row seat to redemption—in two people.

When you recommend a counselor, be careful not to do a referral-as-handoff. Your shepherding presence as a ministry leader is still needed. Your follow up concern communicates that this person has value and helps assuage the fear that "someone knowing my experience would make me unlovable." As you make a counseling recommendation, say something like:

As much as you are willing, keep me informed of what you're learning and deciding. What you're facing is hard. I would like to learn alongside you so I can be a better pastor for others in similar situations. Again, as much as you are willing and as you are ready, I'd like to help identify people from our church who can walk alongside you on this journey.

You don't have to be an expert on anything—legal matters or traumatic sexual abuse counseling—to be a good pastor or ministry leader. You are free to be as helpful as you are currently equipped to be. Your church member will be grateful to have a pastor and church willing to care for them in this way.

KEY POINTS OF THIS LESSON

- Disclosing sexual abuse takes courage and we should honor that courage.
- The report of sexual abuse against a minor or of an abuser who has access to minors should be reported; this is a legal mandate, therefore a matter of obeying Romans 13:1–6.
- When walking with an adult victim of sexual abuse, they should know they have our support in taking whatever legal steps serves them best, and we should connect them with someone experienced in helping victims make those decisions.

FOLLOW UP RESOURCES

- Printable PDF: "Guidelines for Reporting Child Abuse or Neglect" by Brad Hambrick; http://bradhambrick.com/wp-content/uploads/2014/06/Guidelines-for-Reporting-Child-Abuse-and-Neglect.pdf

- Article: "Tamar Listens to Psalm 61: A Reflection on Misused Spiritual Authority" by Brad Hambrick; http://bradhambrick.com/tamarpsalm61/

- Article: "For Pastors: 8 Questions to Vet Potential Counseling Referral Sources" by Brad Hambrick; http://bradhambrick.com/vetcounselors/

- Article: "For Pastors: How to Find a Good Counselor in [Name of City]?" by Brad Hambrick; http://bradhambrick.com/findacounselor/

- Article Series: Sexual Abuse in Marriage: Part 1, Part 2, and Part 3, by Darby Strickland

  Part 1: https://www.ccef.org/resources/blog/sexual-abuse-in-marriage
  Part 2: https://www.ccef.org/resources/blog/sexual-abuse-in-marriage-the-power-of-confusion
  Part 3: https://www.ccef.org/resources/blog/sexual-abuse-in-marriage-the-power-of-confusion

- Article: "9 Ways to Protect Your Children from Sexual Abuse" by Justin Holcomb; http://justinholcomb.com/2015/08/11/9-ways-to-protect-your-children-from-sexual-abuse/

Books

- *On the Threshold of Hope* by Diane Langberg

- *Counseling Survivors of Sexual Abuse* by Diane Langberg

- *The Spiritual Impact of Sexual Abuse* (minibook) by Diane Langberg

- *Bringing Christ to Abused Women* (minibook) by Diane Langberg

- *Rid of My Disgrace* by Justin Holcomb

- *Protecting the Gift: Keeping Children and Teenagers Safe (and Parents Sane)* by Gavin DeBecker

- *God Made All of Me* (children's book) by Justin and Lindsy Holcomb

- *On Guard: Preventing and Responding to Child Abuse at Church* by Deepak Reju

Key Responses to Physical Abuse

Everything that we discussed about sexual abuse applies to physical abuse because *sexual abuse is a form of physical abuse*; the physical assault of sexual abuse should not be missed or minimized.

MINISTRY REFLECTION

How does thinking of sexual abuse as a form of physical abuse help you understand the transferable principles in how each should be handled?

_____

_____

_____

_____

_____

There are several aspects of physical abuse which result in friends, family, and ministry leaders mishandling the initial disclosure of abuse.

The first factor is that by its nature, unless extremely sadistic, physical abuse is episodic. If a victim is beaten for 2 hours each week (which is extreme), that is barely over 1 percent of a 168-hour week. Hence, the abuser says, "Even if it's 'that bad,' it hardly ever happens."

We need to understand both (a) *the nature of abuse* and (b) *the impact of physical abuse.* To use a metaphor about the nature of physical abuse, physical abuse requires the kind of attention that drinking and driving receives. Every occurrence is dangerous enough to warrant attention, and episodes don't have to be frequent enough to be considered "addiction level" to merit strong action.

On the impact of physical abuse, again using a metaphor, physical abuse has an impact more like a concussion than the cancer-causing effects of smoking tobacco over time. The complex and disorienting effects of abuse can occur from a single event and be lasting; it does not require the cumulative effect of repeated behaviors. Victims are sometimes only beaten once to establish control and compliance.

HEAR FROM THE EXPERTS

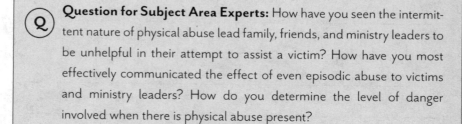

Question for Subject Area Experts: How have you seen the intermittent nature of physical abuse lead family, friends, and ministry leaders to be unhelpful in their attempt to assist a victim? How have you most effectively communicated the effect of even episodic abuse to victims and ministry leaders? How do you determine the level of danger involved when there is physical abuse present?

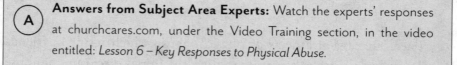

Answers from Subject Area Experts: Watch the experts' responses at churchcares.com, under the Video Training section, in the video entitled: *Lesson 6 – Key Responses to Physical Abuse.*

Chris Moles: Several years ago while teaching at a conference in Indiana I saw something I had never seen before. It was an entire train . . . in motion. Now I know that doesn't sound all that significant but where I'm from (West Virginia) you never see the entire train. We have far too many obstructions like mountains, rivers, and winding terrain. I bring that up because cases of abuse are similar in that you rarely see the entire train; that is, we only catch glimpses of the abuse. We rarely hear of every incident, and will never really comprehend the total impact of abuse. That is one of the reasons many definitions of abuse highlight the existence of a pattern of abusive behavior.

When I have seen cases mismanaged in either the church or the culture, one of the most common elements is a focus on a single incident or an event. This event-oriented approach can limit our vision and enable the abuser by narrowing his responsibility to confessing and repenting of one act, or one specific tactic, leaving the rest of the abuse train, as it were, continuing down the track. I often say that if we only address the event, incident, or presenting problem we risk empowering "polite" abusers who commit more covert, or even respectable sins.

The odds are good that if an abuser is committing acts of physical or sexual abuse than he most likely has escalated from other abusive forms of control. Gathering information about the whole of the relationship and in particular his abuses of power to exercise control are essential to the process. Physical force should always be seen as dangerous and potentially lethal as abuse tends to escalate. Acts such as the presence of weapons, the abuse of pets, strangulation, as well as, threats of suicide or homicide all indicate imminent danger/lethality.

Leslie Vernick: When someone reports physical abuse of any degree, it's crucial that you understand this important dimension—if not you will miss the bigger picture.

Physical abuse in marriage is not about hitting or slapping someone. Physical abuse happens for one purpose: control. An abuser's behavior becomes physical in order to more fully dominate, intimidate, and bully the victim.

However, even without laying a hand on the victim, there may be episodes of intimidating behavior like breaking furniture or punching holes in walls, veiled threats of violence like wearing a holster and gun around the house or threats of violence directed toward pets, children, and treasured mementos that communicate clearly to the victim—I can and will hurt you and what's important to you if I need to.

This "power over" dynamic is not biblical leadership or headship and has a huge negative impact on marriage as well as assaults the very God given dignity of the other.

The writer of Proverbs describes the safety and trust embodied in a good marriage. He writes, "He trusts her to do him good, not harm all the days of his life." Marriage must be a relationship of safety and trust if it is going to be viable long term. Romans 13 reminds us that Love does no harm.

It's important to recognize that physical abuse alone is never sufficient to gain long-term control over another adult. Therefore when you become aware of any kind of physical abuse, however infrequent or minor it may appear, look for other forms of abuse also

For example, there are probably overt abusive behaviors such as threats and/or verbal battering, but also ask about more covert hidden behaviors like mind games, denying one's reality, deceit, and attitudes of entitlement. These covert behaviors are not always fully recognized or defined as abusive, even by the victim.

For example, a husband can exert a lot of power over his wife by not allowing her any say regarding the family money, how it's used, where it's spent, or even how to access it. He can manipulate and confuse her by misusing headship and submission passages, twisting the scriptures to justify his attitude of entitlement without using any physical force.

When there has been physical violence or threats of violence, you need to have a quick way to assess for danger because physical abuse tends to escalate in frequency and severity over time.

Below are nine indicators that increase a victim's level of danger. Any one or combination of these nine indicators requires a need for immediate safety planning.

D—Divorce or separation

A—Alcohol and Drug use

N—Narcissistic tendencies or disordered personality of the abuser

G—Guns or weapons in the home

E—Entitled attitudes and behaviors

R—Rebellious/ history of being unwilling to obey authority figures.

O—Other violent behavior (past history of abuse, violence with pets, road rage)

U—Unstable mental health history

S—Suicidal or homicidal threats or history

If you see any of these nine indicators, please contact your local domestic violence shelter or call 1-800-799-SAFE to consult with an experienced domestic violence advocate that can help you with safety planning.

A second factor that contributes to the mishandling of abuse is the way abusers self-protect—usually by threatening victims to be silent (i.e., "no one will believe you" or "you can't take care of yourself") or tearful apology. *Threats lead victims to remain silent* and *tears lead to confusion* over the nature of repentance.

Threats: When ministry leaders ask, "How long has this been going on?" a response of, "a long time" can lead them to believe this must not be "that bad." After all, wouldn't the victim have spoken sooner? But this response misunderstands the impact that an abuser's threats can have.

The power differential that made the abuse possible in the first place makes the threats more powerful. If you don't understand the impact of power differentials, you will have a very hard time understanding the impact and aftermath of abuse.

Tears: The context of physical abuse is usually love: marriage, or a dating relationship. It is love that allows people to get close enough to hurt us. The victim wants to believe that their abuser loves them. When a victim sees an abuser get to a certain level of anger during an episode of abuse, and then get to a similar level of sadness after it is over, it is assumed that "repentance" has occurred. But, even when sincere, sadness can only reveal remorse, not repentance, because repentance involves actual change. Change is not about "understanding what I did wrong" or feeling particular emotions of sadness. It's about the willingness to defer the use of power and control when expectations are not met.

MINISTRY REFLECTION

Imagine being an abused spouse or child. You don't know when abuse will or won't occur. When you respond to your abuser with fear, they accuse you of being unforgiving or weird. They appeal to the majority of the time when no abuse occurs as evidence that you're exaggerating. They appeal to nice things they've done to make it seem like your fear is slandering them. Try to put into words how "crazy" this would begin to make you feel.

_____

_____

_____

_____

_____

A **third factor** that leads to mishandling physical abuse in Christian circles is, surprisingly, *humility—identifying with the sin of others as no worse than my own.* We've all had moments when our anger has gotten the better of us. But let's examine these two phrases "physical abuse" and "our anger has gotten the better of us." Are those the same? Even if we can't articulate all the differences, intuitively we know there is a difference.

We cannot treat rudeness (dishonor) and abuse (damaging or dangerous behaviors) as if they are synonyms. Yes, Matthew 5 tells us that they exist on the same spectrum of sinful emotion and emerge from the same idolatrous heart described in James 4. But we cannot allow our humility or insecurity about how we wish we had handled past situations better to prevent us from making a wise assessment to protect a victim of abuse.

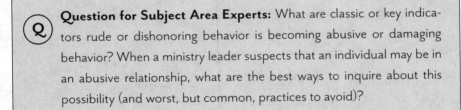

HEAR FROM THE EXPERTS

Q **Question for Subject Area Experts:** What are classic or key indicators rude or dishonoring behavior is becoming abusive or damaging behavior? When a ministry leader suspects that an individual may be in an abusive relationship, what are the best ways to inquire about this possibility (and worst, but common, practices to avoid)?

A **Answers from Subject Area Experts:** Watch the experts' responses at churchcares.com, under the Video Training section, in the video entitled: *Lesson 6 – Key Responses to Physical Abuse.*

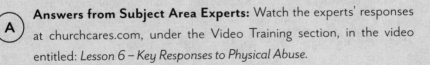

Leslie Vernick: Let's be honest, any one of us can be rude and dishonoring in our language, attitudes, or actions. James 3:2 says we all stumble in many ways.

Because we can all relate to blowing it in our own relationships, we hate to judge someone else as abusive. But there are some critical differences between an ordinary sinner and an abusive person's tactics.

First, when a spiritually healthy yet still sinful person crosses the line, has done something deceptive, mean spirited, or hurtful to someone he or she loves, the Holy Spirit convicts your conscious that you've sinned. We don't feel entitled, justified, or blame the other person for what we did.

Second, when a healthy person crosses the line and hurts someone they love, even if they don't recognize that behavior as abusive, when their loved one tells them OUCH, that hurt, we don't ignore it, or minimize it or mock their pain. Instead we respond with genuine sorrow and repentance and make every effort to not repeat that behavior in the future.

Third, close people in our life feel safe to give us feedback about our attitudes and actions without fearing more abuse.

But that's not the pattern with someone in a relationship with an abuser.

First, there is a lack of personal responsibility for wrongdoing. Instead there is repeated defensiveness, minimizing, excuse-making, and blame shifting. "It's your fault I acted that way. If only you wouldn't make me so mad, or do what I want, this wouldn't have happened."

Second, the victim is not free to honestly talk about his or her feelings or the impact of the abuse without incurring more abuse. As a result, victims tend to become more and more isolated because of having to lie and pretend just to keep the abuse secret or the abuser calm.

Third, even when there is disclosure of abuse, the relationship history shows no long-term change. There may be repeated promises to change but there is no significant change in attitude or action.

Over the years I've received many phone calls from small group leaders in churches who have observed unhealthy and potentially abusive dynamics in a marriage during small group time. They've noticed bruises shaped like fingerprints on a woman's arm or that a husband or wife is cautious about responding to a question the group leader asks.

If you suspect that someone is being abused, it's perfectly appropriate to initiate a private conversation with her or him. You can simply ask, "Are you okay? I've noticed you're not yourself, or you seem nervous to speak up during small group." "Is everything alright at home?"

She or he probably will not be truthful at first, but by initiating that discussion, you've told them that you are willing to hear their story. When they're ready, you might be the very first person they feel safe enough to tell.

One huge mistake some churches have made is assuming marriage counseling is the best treatment option when abuse is disclosed. It is not. That only reinforces the abuser's mind-set that it is someone else's fault he or she behaves that way.

Remember, safety and care for the victim of abuse is your highest priority right now, not repairing their marriage. That comes later if and only when the abuser takes full responsibility for the abuse and has learned to handle his or her frustrations and disappointments in new ways.

Mika Edmondson: In Mark 10:42, Jesus revealed the main characteristics of abusive relationships. He said to His disciples "You know that those who are considered rulers of the Gentiles lord it over them." The Greek word *katakurieuo* translated "lord it over" means more than a simple exercise of authority. It specifically means using authority against a person's interest, to push them downwards and control them. This is an important key to distinguishing between an unhealthy relationship, and an abusive one. Unhealthy relationships still have relative equality and mutuality. However, when one person seeks "to lord over" another, to have power and control over them, the relationship has turned abusive. Abuse can take many different forms (physical, verbal, emotional, spiritual, sexual, and even cultural); however, the common threads are control and fear.

The wrong kind of intervention can put victims in serious danger. Some of the most common mistakes church leaders make when encountering abuse are:

1. **The non-response.** This simply turns a blind eye to abuse, excusing it, minimizing it, or denying it and so leaving victims to continue to endure the cycle of abuse. When we suspect abuse, we must take immediate action, even if that action is consulting with someone who has the experience to help us assess the situation and know how to respond.

2. **The over-response.** This is the opposite pole of non-intervention. This is when church leaders hastily charge into an abusive situation believing that a confrontation will bring about change an abuser into repentance. Since abusers often take their frustrations out on their victims in private, this usually makes things much worse for the victim in the short term by putting them in harm's way and in the long term by modeling to the abuser that intimation is the key to control. When an abuser is confronted unexpectedly, this can become deeply dangerous for the person doing the intervention, especially if the abuser has access to a firearm. Often times, victims of abuse are struggling with their own feelings about their abuse. They may not be ready to confront the issue. In some cases, a hasty intervention can tempt victims to become defensive of their abuser and even shut leadership out of their lives.

3. **The "lone ranger" response.** This response does not make use of the congregation and trained experts in caring for the victim. Often female victims feel more comfortable disclosing abuse to another woman with whom they have a close relationship. While maintaining confidences, it's helpful to employ the gifts of female saints who can ask wise questions. Here are some phrases that I've found helpful. In a non-intrusive and discreet way, pastors or another trusted person can say to a victim:

   - I've noticed _____, are you okay? Is something going on?
   - It seems like talking about _____ can be really upsetting, do you want to talk about it?
   - How can I support you?

   _____

When we see that rudeness has given way to abuse, we must go from assessment to action. The most difficult situations are those where the victim is unwilling, at least at the moment, to make any changes in the relationship. But let's talk about the ideal scenario before we consider a context where the victim is vacillating in their response.

Regardless of whether the victim wants to take steps to pursue safety, there are two powerful things you can do as a ministry leader. First, you can *believe the victim*. "Innocence until proven guilty" is the appropriate legal standard, but you are a ministry leader, not a judge or investigator. We take the posture of 1 Corinthians 13:7, "love believes all things," until there is evidence to the contrary.

Second, you can *connect the victim with counseling resources*. The proper expression of humility in ministry is to know our limits. An experienced abuse counselor or social worker is better able to assess the degree of safety concern. Any effective pastoral ministry builds from a foundation of safety for the victim.

Third, and this is where a victim is sometimes is indecisive, *you can help them develop a safety plan*. The outline of a safety plan is included in the follow up resources. If you are inexperienced at this, you can call a domestic abuse hot line with the victim and support them in processing what they learn. We don't have to have all the answers to be a good pastor. Even if the victim is unsure about enacting the safety plan, having a plan will help them respond with greater intentionality in moments when it is needed.

HEAR FROM THE EXPERTS

Question for Subject Area Experts: What are the keys to developing a good safety plan? What are some of the most overlooked aspects of a good safety plan? What are indicators that a situation is too dangerous and something more substantive than a safety plan is needed? How do we make sure the church's involvement is an asset when a situation is this volatile?

Answers from Subject Area Experts: Watch the experts' responses at churchcares.com, under the Video Training section, in the video entitled: *Lesson 6 – Key Responses to Physical Abuse.*

Darby Strickland: The best safety plan is both comprehensive and one that a victim will implement. There are many helpful documents that can assist in planning, but it is the victim who ultimately has to implement it. Often times, the oppressed need help seeing God's heart for them—many wonder, *Am I sinning by leaving?—even temporarily?* We serve victims well if we locate places in Scripture where God's people fled danger. They need to see fleeing danger as wise and biblical so that they are able to do so when it is prudent.

Even when danger is present, some victims are not ready to separate for their safety, but we can teach them various ways to respond by suggesting strategies for de-escalating, leaving the home or room when there is conflict, or even calling the police. It is common for an oppressed spouse to take months to be ready to act, they have much to lose and fear, so do not tire of reminding them that they are in danger. Keep rehearsing and refining the plan with them.

Fleeing abuse is the most dangerous time for victims, and our inexperience could be costly for them; involve well-trained people, and utilize local resources to help. Be sure to keep any plans protected and secret. In a church setting this often means keeping the circle very small. Taking action first, then informing the broader leadership.

Good safety plans will take into account potential cyber monitoring and stalking; have a packing list that includes legal documents and medications, and address the safety of victims at home and at work. Legal counsel might need to be consulted for potential legal issues—especially those related to child custody. Be sure to take into account pets, which is a common barrier to people seeking their own protection. Continue to work with victims to create a comprehensive plan that they are willing to implement. Look for ways that your church can support them logistically and with resources.

Andrea Munford: Ministry leaders need to be aware that when a victim leaves an abusive situation, it is usually the most dangerous time in a relationship. A victim will often need resources or protection beyond what the church is able to give.

It's difficult for someone who is not familiar with the dynamics of abuse, power, and control to recognize when a situation has reached a dangerous level. And no one can accurately predict what may quickly cause an offender or a situation to escalate. A situation could move quickly from what seems like a minor or isolated incident to an encounter that could put the entire church community at risk. It's important to make sure that law enforcement and experienced advocates are involved in safety planning, as they will not only have resources but they may also have additional information about the offender that ministry leaders are not aware of.

There are often also barriers to a victim leaving an abusive relationship: fear for safety for themselves and others, financial concerns, worry over family members and friends taking sides, or even the feeling that they are responsible for the abuser's actions so they should stay and endure.

Recognizing these barriers can help ministry leaders know what resources are needed and where to seek help if the needs go beyond what the church can offer.

———————

Let's ask an important question: "Why are we, as ministry leaders, often hesitant to take these steps?" A common answer is, "We don't want to be responsible for a divorce." Let's wrestle with our reasoning for a moment.

God created marriage and, therefore, marriage is good. Those things that destroy marriage are, in some way, bad. But if a marriage marked by abuse ends in divorce, what really destroyed the marriage? Was it a safety plan? Or your advisement toward one? No. If pursuing safety results in divorce, that only confirms how dangerous the marriage actually was.

Let's consider a parallel example. If someone under appropriate church discipline accuses the church of being legalistic or arbitrary, this doesn't mean that the church is responsible for the consequences of their sin. The *member* is responsible for ending a covenant relationship with the church, not the pastor who took proper measures. Yet, the unruly member would want us to think that their removal and subsequent "divorce from the church" is the pastor's fault. An abusive spouse would want us to think the same about their marital divorce.

MINISTRY REFLECTION

Use the parallel example of an unrepentant adulterer blaming the church for their isolation after they were non-cooperative and unrepentant during church discipline. You could grieve the condition of their soul without owning consequences of their choices. How is that similar to an abuse situation? If a church enacts its God-given, protective role in the lives of one of its members by creating a safety plan, and that course of action eventually leads to divorce, how would you handle the accusation that it's the church's fault?

_____

_____

_____

_____

_____

The reality is, if a marriage involving abuse is able to be restored, the abusive spouse will eventually be grateful for their spouse pursuing safety. *A genuine believer is more concerned about their own abusive behavior than the embarrassment that comes with the opportunity to repent.* Anyone who abandons a marriage because their abuse is known needs their church to help them see the condition of their soul.

As with good, restorative church discipline, those who are genuinely saved will come to say, "Thank you! I was miserable when I was abusive. I was mad when my church found out. I thought your initial actions were *against* me, but they were *for* me and my family. Now I can see that. Thank you!" While this response is not as frequent as we would like, it is the only response to abuse over which we can rejoice, and ensuring safety is the only appropriate first step towards this goal.

KEY POINTS OF THIS LESSON

- There are many reasons why family, friends, and ministry leaders misconstrue physical abuse.
- When we hear of physical abuse, our first three responses are (1) to believe the victim, (2) to connect the victim to experienced resources, and (3) help them create a safety plan.
- We must denounce the idea that the pursuit of safety is the reason for divorce.

FOLLOW UP RESOURCES

- Article: "How to Develop a Safety Plan for Domestic Violence" by Brad Hambrick; http://bradhambrick.com/safetyplan/

- Article: "What Is a Safety Plan?" from National Domestic Violence Hotline; https://www.thehotline.org/help/path-to-safety/

- Article: "Making a Safety Plan" by Justin and Lindsay Holcomb; http://justinholcomb.com/2014/05/24/making-a-safety-plan/

- Article: "Power-Control Relationships vs. Mutual Honor Relationships" by Brad Hambrick; http://bradhambrick.com /power-control-relationships-vs-mutual-honor-relationships/

- Small Group Leader Video: "How Do We, as a Small Group, Walk Well with Someone Considering Divorce Because of Adultery or Abuse?" by Brad Hambrick; http://bradhambrick. com/sgdivorce/

- PDF: "Domestic Violence Safety Assessment Tool" from NSW Government; http://www.domesticviolence.nsw.gov.au/__data/ assets/file/0020/301178/DVSAT.pdf

What Happens When You Call CPS? Don't Avoid What You Don't Understand

You may have read the series of books by C. S. Lewis called The Chronicles of Narnia. In *The Magician's Nephew*, two children find themselves in the world of Charn staring at a strange bell with the inscription:

> "Make your choice, adventurous Stranger,
> Strike the bell and bide the danger,
> Or wonder, till it drives you mad,
> What would have followed if you had."[1]

In this brief poem, Lewis invites his readers to wrestle with the human response to unknown outcomes. You'll have to read the book to find out what happens next in Narnia, but in this lesson we want to explore the "unknown outcome" of what happens when you call CPS. We don't want uncertainty to be the reason we don't take action to help an abused or neglected child.

---

1. C. S. Lewis, *The Magician's Nephew* in The Chronicles of Narnia series (New York: Harper Collins, 2001, 35.

MINISTRY REFLECTION

How do you respond to uncertainty? Do you tend towards taking action or staying passive? If you had to guess, what happens after a phone call is made to CPS? What do you fear happening after you make a call to CPS?

_____

_____

_____

_____

_____

BEFORE THE PHONE CALL

Let's review what happens before you make a call to CPS. *The simple standard is that you have a "reasonable suspicion" that a child is experiencing abuse or neglect.* A phone call to CPS is a way to get an experienced second opinion from someone with the authority to intervene if your suspicion is potentially valid.

DURING THE PHONE CALL

When you speak to CPS, let them know you are calling to report your concerns of neglect or abuse. The case worker will begin to ask you a series of questions, from a structured interview form. A link to the North Carolina version of this structured interview can be found here: https://www2.ncdhhs.gov/info/olm/forms/dss/dss-1402-ia.pdf. You should ask a social worker from your state to share the version for your area.

The purpose of the structured interview is to ensure the conversation covers key subjects. Your goal is to answer the questions *as best you can.*

Don't be alarmed if your answer to some of the questions is "I don't know." You are simply giving CPS the information you have as a starting place for them to vet the concern.

These forms are divided into categories: physical abuse, sexual abuse, emotional abuse, substance abuse, abandonment, etc. Don't let it unsettle you that some of the questions explore areas that are not relevant to the situation you are reporting. CPS is just following protocol.

AFTER THE PHONE CALL

After a report is received, the CPS worker you spoke with will talk to their supervisor to decide whether the report will be accepted for assessment. This means two case workers have to deem the case worthy of further investigation in order for action to be taken. Even if CPS does not accept your report for investigation, this does not mean it was wrong or unwise for you to make the report.

As the reporter, you should know that your identity is anonymous. CPS will not reveal any identifying information about you in their investigation. However, CPS will tell the family what the allegations are and use exact phrases from their report during their interviews.

CPS will either respond immediately, within 24 hours, or within 72 hours depending on their level of concern. CPS should send you a notice, in the form of letter, of the outcome of their case within 30 days.

We are discussing the ideal or standard protocols for CPS. As an institution run by humans, CPS does not always operate according to its ideals any more than the church always operates according to our ideals. Don't let frustrations with one case cause you to neglect your responsibilities with a future case.

Be sure to get the CPS worker's name and the case number so you can verify your report, if needed.

HEAR FROM THE EXPERTS

 Question for Subject Area Experts: What are the best ways for a ministry leader to continue pastoral care after a report to CPS has been made? What is helpful and what gets in the way? How should ministry leaders respond during the investigation phase when the parent/child or victim/alleged perpetrator are both members of their church?

 Answers from Subject Area Experts: Watch the experts' responses at churchcares.com, under the Video Training section, in the video entitled: *Lesson 7 – What Happens When You Call CPS? Don't Avoid What You Don't Understand.*

Andrea Munford: Ministry leaders should recognize that after CPS has been notified, it is important to continue support to a victim and their caretaker by ensuring that the victim still feels welcomed by the church community. Many victims, especially children, will feel like they have done something wrong or that they have gotten someone in trouble.

Though leaders will need to limit the number of people who know about a situation, it's helpful to prepare church leaders who can give similar support and messaging, care ministry, children's ministry, and security teams, for example, so that a child feels supported and safe at the church. Be mindful that sometimes information does get spread through a church, which could negatively impact the child's social environment, sometimes even manipulated by the offender. Church leaders need to be aware that this could happen and have a plan to address it.

It's important to monitor situations where an offender may be seeking out care or treatment at the church, attending services, or participating in other events, so that contact with a victim or their family member does not occur. Communicate to the offender that they are not to be on the church premises. Be prepared that you may have to offer to meet with the offender at scheduled times outside normal church activity hours. Make every attempt not to change the schedule or activities of the victim, as this could further traumatize them and leave them feeling they are being punished for speaking out against the abuse. Of course, if there is a safety concern, it would be appropriate for the victim not to maintain a schedule that an offender is familiar with. Involve law enforcement and/or child protective service professionals to assist with safety planning.

Karla Siu: It's important for pastors and ministers to stay in communication with victims after a report has been made. Remember that it takes tremendous courage to speak up and take these first steps. Letting them know that you are there and walking through this situation with them is therefore invaluable.

How you walk alongside will look differently based on the personality, age, and unique needs of the victim. You should feel free to ask about these preferences directly, so that they can let you know what they need. Your question about what they need may be the first time they've been asked this, so be patient with them if they don't initially know what to say.

It's helpful as ministers to remember that victims will go through different kinds of emotions ranging from sadness and relief to fear, worry, and even anger, etc. It's also common for victims to experience the fallout of a situation and wonder whether they should've said anything in the first place. As we all know, change is difficult and can feel disorienting, particularly in the initial stages. So encourage them and reassure them.

An effective way to reassure someone is by reciting back to them their reason for taking this leap of faith. It's important not to rush victims through the confusion and all the conflicting emotions that they will experience. Gently point them again towards the hope that allowed them to take that bold first step. Remember that being heard, listened to, respected, etc., are the good soil necessary for the seeds of hope we plant to flourish. These quiet, yet powerful acts of love can restore a victim's personhood and value over time.

IF THE REPORT IS ACCEPTED FOR INVESTIGATION

When CPS begins their assessment with families, they take one of two approaches:

1. *An investigative assessment* is the response *that involves a clear risk of serious harm to the child.* Investigative assessments are often done in collaboration with law enforcement.
2. The more frequent approach CPS uses is *a family assessment* approach. This approach is *used for lower risk situations that still merit investigation.* In this approach, the first contact with the family is typically to call and schedule a time to meet with them.

Step One: Safety Plan

After CPS initiates a case, they typically discuss concerns with the family and put a safety plan in place. This is *a signed agreement* with the family about how they will ensure the safety of the child. Also at this time, CPS will attempt to connect the family with resources relevant to family's needs.

This is an area where the church can be an immense asset. Ask to see the safety plan, because children or student ministry leaders may need to be informed of limitations on who can pick up the children. Offer to help with childcare, supervised visitation, or other ways of ensuring family safety.

HEAR FROM THE EXPERTS

Q **Question for Subject Area Experts:** When CPS is helping a family, what are the best ways you've seen churches be involved in the safety plan phase? What complex shepherding needs arise for which the church is uniquely positioned and equipped to meet?

A **Answers from Subject Area Experts:** Watch the experts' responses at churchcares.com, under the Video Training section, in the video entitled: *Lesson 7 – What Happens When You Call CPS? Don't Avoid What You Don't Understand.*

Chris Moles: Safety plans are essential with any abuse intervention. They are a key ingredient to success. As we partner with agencies, it is imperative that we view safety as our priority. Sometimes in our desire to see reconciliation or to promote forgiveness (all wonderful things), we have undermined safety by rushing ahead and in doing so we may bypass the good gifts God has given us through skilled professionals and people helpers.

When safety is the priority and we practice patience, we can step back and see all the conditions and expectations in a given case. Shepherding is difficult enough in isolation, sharing responsibility brings with it distinct temptations as well as unique opportunities. Rather than competing with agencies and people helpers, I have found it helpful to view them as a person of peace, regardless of their personal conviction. Remember, if safety is the priority, then here is a partner to lock arms with for the safety of victim.

Relying on court officials, therapists, social workers, etc., can free you to function best in a shepherding capacity. Speaking of shepherding, there are opportunities throughout the intervention process in which we can serve the victim, perpetrator, and case workers.

First, is in how we respond to the abuse. A willingness to participate in the comfort of the victim through prayer, support, friendship, and safety are essential. In the same way, a willingness to confront the sin of abuse and hold a high standard communicate what we value loud and clear. Too many times I have seen churches value a false sense of peace over actual peace and safety by treating the parties equally, trying not to take sides, attempting to rush reconciliation, and in turn isolating the victim more while placating the abuser.

Separate paths of discipleship are warranted as we are not addressing a relationship problem, like a child to a parent or a husband to a wife, but the effect of sin committed against the victim, and the necessary but good consequences for sin applied to the abuser. Practically speaking, there are numerous ways in which you and your church can serve the victim through the natural benefits of community. Offering rides to appointments, offering facilities for supervised visitation, providing meals when needed, honoring court orders in regards to no, or limited contact, and the list goes on.

If a Child Is at Greater Risk

When CPS finds that a child's safety continues to remain at-risk, they can remove a child from the home. Besides the priority of keeping families together, taking children away from their parents is a complicated, expensive, and time-consuming task that CPS wants to avoid as much as possible. If a child is placed outside of their home, it is only because CPS has found the parents non-compliant with the safety plan and there is no way to guarantee the child's safety in the home.

CPS tries to keep children as close to their current living situation as possible; close to their current homes, in the same school, and in contact with their family. This is where church members, who are in the same community, can be of great assistance by serving as foster families.

HEAR FROM THE EXPERTS

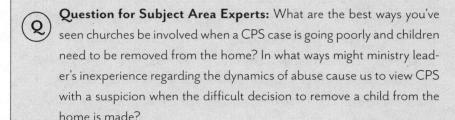

Question for Subject Area Experts: What are the best ways you've seen churches be involved when a CPS case is going poorly and children need to be removed from the home? In what ways might ministry leader's inexperience regarding the dynamics of abuse cause us to view CPS with a suspicion when the difficult decision to remove a child from the home is made?

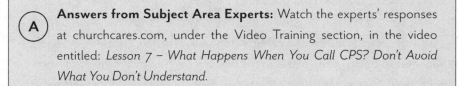

Answers from Subject Area Experts: Watch the experts' responses at churchcares.com, under the Video Training section, in the video entitled: *Lesson 7 – What Happens When You Call CPS? Don't Avoid What You Don't Understand.*

Diane Langberg: Ministry does not stop just because there are legal issues or the state is involved. Christians often do not want the civil authorities to be part of the equation because they rightly believe the family to be a God-ordained institution and therefore under the arm of the church. However, there are also laws that govern marriage and family and God calls us to obey them. The sexual abuse of a child, the rape of an adult, or the battering of a human being are all against the law—both man and God's. We need the state to enforce these laws for the safety and care of the vulnerable. To refuse this is to turn from something God has called us to do in His Word. When a family is broken up by the state, it is merely turning the light on an already very broken and damaging home. So a little girl may be removed from the home (which grieves us), but it may also mean it is the first time in her young life she has been safe in her bed at night.

Many in ministry have never been taught or read about abuse. Sadly, there is often much wrongdoing going on behind closed doors even in the Christian world. Those who look fine on Sundays can be doing great damage to those in the home. When pastors do not understand the levels of deception involved in such behavior they have little understanding of the deeply ingrained, habituated behavior, supported by those lies. "The desire to help without knowledge is not good and he who hurries to act will do damage" (Prov. 19:2). When abuse in the home has come to the light, that means that the cancer has been exposed. And as in the physical world, treatment for such things is slow and grueling and feels hurtful. However, if that treatment is not done, more damage and eventually death will follow.

Having the authorities involved in these areas does not under any circumstances undermine the work of the church. In fact, loving care and shepherding is sorely needed in these circumstances. Life has been turned upside down by the sin of another. A spouse is in prison, children have been damaged by an abusive and untrustworthy parent, and life is completely changed. Steady consistent care by the church providing support and some predictability is critical. A little boy who needs someone to show up for his games, or a girl who needs someone at her concert, or a wife who has never been responsible for the bills and who now must work and figure out the bank account—they all need the people of the church to walk with them with consistency and care. It is not a path anyone should walk alone.

Mika Edmondson: When abuse occurs, and CPS makes the hard decision to remove a child from a home, it's very easy to lose sight of the real crisis. The real crisis is not CPS's decision to remove a child from danger. Rather, the real crisis is the abuse that necessitated the removal in the first place.

Unhealthy responses tend to confuse these issues. For instance, if church leadership treats separation as a greater crisis than the abuse itself, they may resist the counsel of CPS and make an already difficult process even more excruciating. Ministry leaders may unwittingly undermine a family's cooperation with CPS by disparaging the decision to remove the child. Pastors do well to avoid speaking of the decision to bring a child to a safe home as "unnecessary" or "unfortunate." Throughout the Scripture, God is described as a "maw-oze" (Ps. 43:2; Prov. 10:29) literally, a refuge, safe haven, and place of safety. When an abused child finally reaches a place of safety, this becomes a matter of praise rather than lament. We must remember that child abuse is a form of domestic violence carried out against a victim without the ability to self-advocate or escape. CPS is often the only means they have of doing so.

Another unhealthy response occurs when church leaders blame CPS for the hurt caused by separating a child from his/her family. The hurt that is felt when a child is removed from abuse must be identified as being caused by the abuser's decision to abuse, not CPS's decision to protect. Without downplaying the trauma of losing a child, a pastor can help a family understand and humbly accept the consequences of their pattern of abuse as an act of repentance.

Leaders must resist the temptation to back away from a child simply because they have been removed from a member's home. It may seem awkward, but pastors do well to maintain the pastoral relationship with the child who has been removed. The legal process occurring in the child's life does not take the place of discipleship. When Jesus declared, "Let the little children come to me and do not hinder them, for to such belongs the kingdom of heaven" (Matt. 19:14 ESV). He revealed His great love and concern for children as disciples.

Discipleship must continue in the life of a child even after they are removed from a member's home. That discipleship should not serve as a platform for the parents to express themselves to their child. Rather, this is an opportunity to come alongside a deeply devastated and confused child who has been betrayed by the closest adults in their lives. Pastors must help these "little lambs" to know that God is their safe haven and will provide a safe haven for them against physical harm. Once, a healthy home is found for the child, pastors may help a child give God thanks for having a safe environment.

Finally, as pastors walk alongside abusive adults through losing a child, there are some key mistakes to avoid. Pastors do well to avoid presumptuous assurances of hasty reunions. Since abusive patterns normally take a long time to address, pastors serve families more effectively when they help them understand the depth of the harm they've caused and the amount of time it will take to begin to make things right. Also, when they help them prioritize their maturity in Christ over a hasty reuniting with their child. This means helping adults address abusive attitudes and patterns so that they may turn from them and seek healing. Remember, a hasty reunion may only put a vulnerable child back in harm's way and place a temptation before an abusive adults to continue sinning. Any reconciliation, must come on the heels of a genuine long-term patterns of repentance. Jesus never promised that our earthly families would always remain intact. However, He did promise to be with us through every situation, to strengthen our fight against sin, and to shape us into His image (Rom. 8:28–30).

We know this brief lesson cannot answer all the questions you have about CPS. When a child's safety is at risk, our minds can and should race with questions. If you have more questions, invite a CPS social worker to come to a church staff meeting or volunteer training for a Q&A.

MINISTRY REFLECTION

What lingering questions and emotions do you have about what happens when CPS is involved with a family where there is abuse or neglect of children? Who in your church or community would be able process these questions with you?

_____

_____

_____

_____

_____

The goal of this lesson is to ensure that uncertainty about a process does not create passivity. It will never be "comfortable" when a call to CPS is needed. But at this point you should know enough to call CPS with confidence, understanding what is happening on the other end of the call.

KEY POINTS OF THIS LESSON

- The criterion for calling CPS is a "reasonable suspicion" of abuse or neglect of a child.
- CPS will take you through a standardized interview process and vet the information received by two case workers (the intake worker and their supervisor) to determine if an investigation is needed.

- There are multiple ways it is possible for your church to serve the child and family during the CPS investigation process and afterward.

FOLLOW UP RESOURCES

- Article: "Ten Things Everyone Should Know About Child Protective Services" by We Have Kids; https://wehavekids.com /parenting/InsideCPS

- A 135-page overview of the role of CPS: *Child Protective Services: A Guide for Case Workers*; https://www.childwelfare.gov/pubP-DFs/cps.pdf

- Podcast: "Reporting Abuse" by Julie Lowe (CCEF); https://www. ccef.org/podcast/reporting-abuse-julie-lowe/

- An organization that helps children in unsafe homes: *Safe Families*; https://safe-families.org/about/

Non-Criminal Forms of Abuse (Verbal and Emotional)

What do we mean when we say "non-criminal" abuse? It can be easy to think that all abuse is illegal; or that if something isn't illegal, it's not abuse.

To say that there are forms of abuse which are not illegal *in no way minimizes how wrong these forms of abuse are*. It merely indicates who has jurisdiction over the consequences for these actions: the civil authorities for matters that are illegal, the church for matters that are immoral within their congregation.

It should be noted that there are some forms of verbal abuse which are illegal, such as making terroristic threats. If you are in doubt, you should consult with a law enforcement officer.

MINISTRY REFLECTION

What are other examples of things that are immoral but not illegal? What are things that are legal, but immoral—things that your church would take a strong stance against even if they were allowable by law? Is emotional and verbal abuse on that list?

_____

_____

_____

_____

_____

If you've ever tried to research a definition for emotional, verbal, or psychological abuse, you've doubtless been frustrated. Unfortunately, there is no consensus amongst experts. This doesn't mean emotional abuse doesn't exist, it just means it is hard to objectively define.

Rather than giving a definition, it is more beneficial to describe a constellation of qualities that constitute verbal or emotional abuse.

Control

Humiliation

Manipulation

Intimidation

Contradictory Demands

Lies / Threats

Isolating someone from family and friends

Blame-shifting for things you actually did wrong

Financial: no granting a spouse access to funds or forcing them to
ask for money

Spiritual: making one-sided application of Scripture to demand, control, or condemn

All of these things with the effects of creating fear, shame, and
indecisiveness

The more of these qualities that are present, the more toxic the relationship. Reading the list, each adjective seems clear enough. But imagine
trying to convince someone who doesn't want to admit it, that what they
are doing is actually abusive. Now, imagine your well-being depended on
getting them to admit it and change their pattern of behavior. That is the
life of someone living in an emotionally abusive relationship.

HEAR FROM THE EXPERTS

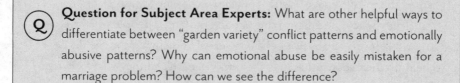

Question for Subject Area Experts: What are other helpful ways to
differentiate between "garden variety" conflict patterns and emotionally
abusive patterns? Why can emotional abuse be easily mistaken for a
marriage problem? How can we see the difference?

Answers from Subject Area Experts: Watch the experts' responses
at churchcares.com, under the Video Training section, in the video
entitled: *Lesson 8 – Non-Criminal Forms of Abuse (Verbal and Emotional).*

Leslie Vernick: Healthy conflict involves two or more people having a different opinion or approach to a problem. Ideally they work together to understand
and to come to a mutually agreeable solution to resolve a problem. Plus, there
is freedom to disagree without fearing a price to pay or being demeaned, disrespected, or degraded in the process.

In an emotionally abusive relationship, that doesn't happen. Words and gestures are used to manipulate, control, punish, and wound. Conflict isn't resolved, it is avoided or blame-shifted. A destructive marriage isn't just difficult or disappointing. It is devastating to the very God-given dignity of the other.

An emotionally destructive relationship is usually not determined by looking at one single episode of sinful behavior which all of us are capable of but rather by looking for pervasive and repetitive patterns of sinful behavior coupled with attitudes of entitlement that result in tearing someone down or inhibiting a spouse's growth.

Many times people helpers, counselors, and pastors get called during a marital crisis. "Pastor, he hit me." Or " Pastor, I found pornography on the computer." Or, "We need help, I just discovered my wife's been having multiple affairs." It's important in these moments to understand that abuse, addictions, and chronic adultery are not marital problems. For sure they cause marital problems, but at their heart, they are serious personal sin issues and must be seen as such for genuine healing to take place.

Truth be told, there are many unhappily married people who love God and don't resort to abusive behavior, sexual addictions, chronic deceit, or cheat on their spouse because their marriage isn't all they wished it were. They know that those behaviors displease God, hurt their testimony, diminish the person that they wanted to be, and hurt their marriage as well as their children.

However an abuser believes he or she is entitled to act out. An abusive person use their marriage and their spouse's flaws as an excuse for their abusive or addictive ways. As ministry leaders, it's important to be mindful of these mind-sets and manipulative tactics to avoid responsibility and shift the blame.

All spouses will disappoint one another at times. In marriage counseling, the healthier spouse will be self-reflective and accept personal responsibility for their personal failures. However, this becomes problematic where abusive patterns are going on. Why? Because the victim will be blamed for the abusers acting out, both by the abuser and sometimes by the pastor or counselor. We counsel the victim, "Don't push his buttons" or "Stop making the abuser mad." Or, "Why can't you be more sexually adventurous or available?"

But that approach only enables the oppressive spouse and validates their abuse. As long as the victim can be blamed and told it's the victim's fault the abuser behaves that way, then the abuser escapes taking personal responsibility for his or her own sinful and destructive behaviors.

Best practices are not to begin with marriage counseling but rather to individually help each person work on their own issues with separate counselors. That may not be your role as the pastor but the work to do is individual work as the first level of treatment.

First, we must address the abusers entitlement attitude and blame-shifting pattern so that the abuser takes full responsibility for his or her own sinful behaviors and attitudes as well as for their own maturity and growth. Second, we need to help the victim understand that she or he is not responsible for the abuser's acting out behavior nor are they to blame for the ways their spouse handles their own emotional distress.

In addition, the victim may need individual counseling to appropriately speak up, stop being a pretender, placater, or people-pleaser, learn how to implement appropriate consequences for grievous and repetitive sin, as well as heal from any trauma wounds that have limited the abused person's ability to function as a healthy individual. If the marriage is to be saved, that work must come later.

Andrea Munford: Abusers are usually manipulative, seen as the "nice guy" or "great husband/father" or "committed to the church/community." This is how an offender grooms people close to them, and close to the victim, to believe they could never be abusive. The abuser presents their spouse as "crazy" or "a bad wife." An abused victim may not recognize the cycle of control they are in. They may have come to believe that the abuse is their fault, or believe when the abuser claims they are crazy.

Research teaches us that there are three sides to everyone's life: Public, Private, and Secret. Understand that what we typically see is someone's public persona, what they choose for us to see, and sometimes a part of their private persona, depending on our relationship with them. But the secret side, a side we all have, is what we typically don't share with others. For most people, there is no intent for deviant or criminal behavior. With offenders, this is where the abusive persona lives, and they make sure to keep others from only seeing the public persona they want us to see.

———————

All of this begs a question, "What is the point of differentiating 'garden variety problems' from emotionally abusive dynamics? Should anything be done differently?" Yes, but in the case of emotional abuse, the answer is not "call the police." So, then, what do we do?

We arrive at an answer by asking three questions:

1. Is the emotionally abusive person present for pastoral care (likely marriage counseling)?
2. Are we only talking to the emotionally abused person?
3. Is the emotionally abusive person a church member?

MINISTRY REFLECTION

Before we engage these three questions, make a few notes on what you anticipate the implications of these three questions would be.

_____

_____

_____

_____

_____

Question One: *Is the emotionally abusive person present for pastoral care?* If the answer is yes, then pastoral counseling needs to become individual rather than marital or familial, and it needs to focus on:

1. raising self-awareness about the nature of the abusive spouse/parent's actions
2. garnering ownership for these actions once they can be acknowledged without minimization
3. developing strategies for dealing with irritating or distressing situations more effectively.

We will discuss this kind of pastoral care more in Lesson 10.

The rationale for discontinuing marriage or family counseling is that relational counseling validates the idea that there is joint responsibility for the abusive behavior. Instruction given to the marriage or family will inevitably be used against the oppressed spouse or children in the home environment resulting in pastoral guidance, inadvertently validating and empowering the abusive behaviors.

Question Two: *Are we only talking to the emotionally abused person?* Often this person feels very stuck. Things are "bad enough" that their home life is undoing them, but things aren't "bad enough" that any legal steps can be taken. They wonder, "Am I exaggerating? Will anyone believe me? Can anything be done?"

In these instances the first two responses to physical abuse are still relevant: believe what the person is saying and connect them with an experienced counselor (if they are willing). However, a vital need that the church is uniquely positioned to fill is *social and spiritual support.* Connecting the individual with a friend who is understanding and supportive in the midst of the relational angst is invaluable.

Prior to disclosing the emotionally abusive dynamics, this person lived in two worlds: home life and everyday life. These two worlds were so different it made them feel crazy. After engaging counseling, the person begins to live in three worlds: home life, everyday life, and counseling (where they feel understood). But a friend, instead of adding a fourth world, is a companion who is aware of each sphere in which the person lives.

HEAR FROM THE EXPERTS

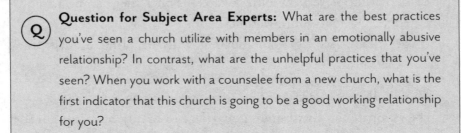

Q **Question for Subject Area Experts:** What are the best practices you've seen a church utilize with members in an emotionally abusive relationship? In contrast, what are the unhelpful practices that you've seen? When you work with a counselee from a new church, what is the first indicator that this church is going to be a good working relationship for you?

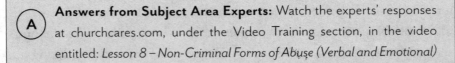

A **Answers from Subject Area Experts:** Watch the experts' responses at churchcares.com, under the Video Training section, in the video entitled: *Lesson 8 – Non-Criminal Forms of Abuse (Verbal and Emotional)*

Chris Moles: First of all, *I love working with churches that approach me for help with a teachable spirit.* By the time a case is referred to me, the church has often exhausted their ministry know-how. In particular, because tactics of emotional abuse rarely carry legal consequences, churches may struggle to properly identify the issue and therefore offer a proper response. So, a teachable team will be willing to learn broader definitions of abuse, dialogue through case studies and literature. They will quickly repent of poor counsel and dangerous recommendations.

Unfortunately, I have encountered some churches who "double-down" on marriage-focused solutions, or consult with me in the hopes that I'll support their agenda that downplays abuse, rather than offer help for the case at hand.

Second, *I'm looking for a justice-minded leadership team.* What I mean by that is a team that understands a commitment to righteousness may require them to commit long hours to the process with potential risks. Confronting abuse will invite criticism, manipulation, slander, and possible relational fallout. Leaders must care more about safety and justice for the victim first and foremost.

Lastly, *I'm looking for hope.* Does the team see redemption as possible, and are they willing to do the hard work of calling the offender to repentance while supporting the victim.

Leslie Vernick: Churches and ministry leaders who use a team approach and have frequent and open communication among team members are my favorite to work with because they have the best possibility for a positive outcome.

In situations of domestic abuse, pastors or small group leaders who have faithfully come alongside the abuser and said, "Hey we love you, but the way you think and behave towards your spouse is not okay. We will do all we can to help you change, but we won't help you continue to lie and pretend, nor will we pressure your spouse to put up with it anymore." There is something life-giving when help is coupled with positive peer pressure.

However, a practice church leaders must be extremely careful of is not to turn the victim of abuse into the villain. Truth be told, there are times that we will like and even believe the accused abuser far more than we like and believe the victim. The accused abuser can be charming, resourceful, a charismatic leader, clever, fun to be around, and may even be a generous financial donor. And the victim appears uncooperative, mistrusting, fearful, angry, and hard-hearted.

For example, sometimes we see the abuser fully cooperating with the process we've put in place. He seems to get it and is working hard to change. On the other hand, the victim is unwilling to participate in marriage counseling. They resist our treatment plan for reconciliation and appear uncooperative.

Before long, what can happen is the true victim of abuse has now been cast in the role of the villain in the situation and the abuser is seen as the victim of an unloving, uncooperative, hard-hearted spouse. Church support and pastoral care rallies around the abuser who is working so hard to reconcile his or her marriage. In the process we've often failed to help the victim process their suffering nor given the abused sufficient time to heal from the trauma. We've pushed reconciling the marriage before the personal healing of the individual. Nor have we allowed the victim sufficient time to test the changed behaviors of the abuser in order to see whether the fruit of repentance is genuine.

Question Three: *Is the emotionally abusive person a church member?* When the emotionally abusive person is a church member, it affords some additional types of intervention that can be wisely engaged.

But to reiterate, *the church should <u>not</u> confront the abuser until the oppressed spouse is ready for it.* Also, a safety plan should already be in place before this kind of meeting is attempted.

When the oppressed spouse is ready, an initial conversation should take place with the allegedly unruly spouse, the concerns should be raised, and their response heard. Only the most tangible examples should be used in this meeting. When weak or subjective examples are used, then those are the ones that will be countered, and by negating the weak examples, the spouse will feel that they have nullified the entire concern and "won the argument" being raised against them.

HEAR FROM THE EXPERTS

Q **Question for Subject Area Experts:** What are best practices in the initial conversation with an emotionally abusive person? How can these interactions be given the best opportunity to succeed? What are the common pitfalls that ministry leaders would need to be aware of? Since oppressors are most often motivated by the desire for control, how might that begin to play out in our interactions with them?

A **Answers from Subject Area Experts:** Watch the experts' responses at churchcares.com, under the Video Training section, in the video entitled: *Lesson 8 – Non-Criminal Forms of Abuse (Verbal and Emotional)*

Chris Moles: One area that I have found helpful to highlight with abusive men is the impact of their abuse. I generally begin by gathering as much data as I can regarding not just the incident at hand but the relationship. I'm looking for the pattern of abuse over the relationship's history.

If you're new to this work, the power and control wheel by Duluth Abuse Intervention Project can be a helpful tool. As you ask questions, be looking for actions that fit in each category such as threats, isolation, or economic abuse. Multiple tactics used over time can give you a greater sense of the scope of abuse, and placing them on a time line can help you see the escalatory nature of abuse.

Once I've gathered relevant info on the behavior, I attempt to connect each behavior to the actual or potential outcome. Because abusers are so eager to manipulate, minimize, or blame, it is easy to be lured into the trap of, "But, I had good intentions." I once worked with a man who had broken his wife's hand. And he passionately tried to convince us that he didn't mean to. The reality is that one's intention doesn't outweigh the impact, and frankly when we do uncover motives we can focus on the sinister nature of abuse rather than the softened claims of the perpetrator.

Darby Strickland: To understand how to help we must understand what is at root. Oppressors usurp God's position and live out life as if they are the one to be worshiped and obeyed. They struggle with deep-seated issues of entitlement and believe they should be the object of others' concern and care. When their expectations are not met, oppressors become punishing and attacking. Abusers are willing to wound others in order to maintain power and control.

The best way to address this sin pattern is to be concrete. Hone in on their particular entitlements and be specific with the sinful punishing behaviors that they use to control others. You might say to them, "When you speak to your wife or daughter, you are harsh, critical, dismissive, or untruthful." You might ask questions like, "Why do you ignore her? Withhold affection? Or ridicule her?" Instead of telling someone they are abusive, which is too broad an accusation, usually making them defensive be as descriptive as possible. For instance, "I see this manipulative fruit coming from your heart—when you told your spouse that what they saw and heard never happened, you left them confused—how did you benefit from their self-doubt?"

Help them see that their behavior does damage and has a purpose, like controlling another for their own comfort. You are looking to bring insight to them in a way that they see their need for repentance and Jesus. Because often oppressors are hard-hearted and believe that they right, they are usually not willing to hear another person's perspective. Prepare for this, bring them many concrete examples that showcase their oppressive entitlements.

Keep in mind abusers will work on you to feel sorry for them—they want you to see their victim as the cause of their torment, and hence their sins as reasonable or excusable. We as empathic people can easily get turned around and wander aimlessly in their maze of self-pity and victimhood. We need to remember what fuels abuse and continue to pursue the unmasking of their entitlements and punishments.

Assuming the concerns prove valid, this becomes a situation where it is important to use a church discipline process like the one discussed in Lesson 2.

Cases of emotional and verbal abuse are notorious for cultivating dozens of renditions of events that perpetually change. Tertiary things are raised to the level of primary things, and primary concerns easily get lost. This is why a structured, documented discipline process is essential.

To prevent unhealthy "teaming" or triangulating of care teams, you should ask that both spouses be willing to allow the disciplinary document (which records the history and the stages of the progress) be shared with anyone from the church from whom they seek guidance or support. This helps to ensure that neither spouse receives bad advice from well-meaning friends because those friends have been told an incomplete or inaccurate version of events. In other words, every person involved should be working with the same information.

This documentation process also addresses a frequent ministry concern regarding separation: *the perceived precedent set for separation within healthier marriages.* Documenting the church discipline process forces the pastoral team to be specific about the severity of sin and the hardness of heart being addressed.

As much as any other lesson in this series, handling this topic well will produce discernment in your church leadership about destructive communication patterns. The assessment skills and self-awareness you gain will serve you well in many other areas of life and ministry.

KEY POINTS OF THIS LESSON

- While all forms of abuse are immoral, not all forms of abuse are illegal.
- When overseeing pastoral care in an emotionally abusive situation, keeping well-documented case notes is essential to alleviate as much confusion as possible.

FOLLOW UP RESOURCES

- Article: "When NOT to Do Marriage Counseling" by Winston Smith; https://www.ccef.org/resources/?fwp_search=When%20 NOT%20to%20Do%20Marriage%20Counseling

- PDF Assessment: "The Emotionally Destructive Relationship" by Leslie Vernick; https://leslievernick.com/pdfs/Relationship-test.pdf

- Blog Series: "Marriage with a Chronically Self-Centered Spouse" by Brad Hambrick; http://bradhambrick.com/selfcenteredspouse/

- Structured Guide & Video: "Restorative Church Discipline Process" by Brad Hambrick; http://bradhambrick.com/?s=Resto rative+Church+Discipline+Process

- Article: "How Abuse Affects You as a Mother" by Darby Strickland; https://www.darbystrickland.com/blog/how-abuse -effects-you-as-a-mother

Pastoral Care After Reporting: Reporting Is *Not* a Ministerial Hand Off

It might be easy to think that once you connect an abused individual to the best-fit social worker, counselor, or law enforcement officer, your pastoral work is done. After all, it is only a matter of time before another crisis emerges in the life of another church member and you have a sermon to write, committee meeting to lead, homebound person to visit, *and* your own family to invest in before then.

Every ministry leader wears an inordinate number of hats. Doubtless, this is why once the appropriate report or referral is made, pastoral care can unintentionally be neglected.

It is easy to think that "church = pastor" when you read the title of this lesson: *Pastoral Care After Reporting.* If that is how you're thinking, your thoughts are likely racing as you wonder, "How am I going to do more?"

It is only a church-as-entire-body that can provide the kind of care an abuse victim needs. In this lesson, we will be thinking of you as the *coordinator* of the church's ministry care; not the sole provider of that care.

MINISTRY REFLECTION

It is safe to assume two things about you. First, *you care*, or you wouldn't be going through this material. Second, *you're tired*. There is so much brokenness in our world to tend to, and often ministry leaders are exhausted by trying to meet all the needs that exist in their church and beyond. Go ahead and put your "I can't do more" thoughts down on paper. If you feel like you're nearing burnout, talk to someone or visit bradhambrick.com/burnout for additional guidance.

_____

_____

_____

_____

_____

When we make a referral to a good-fit professional, what have we done? We've added needed player(s) to our ministry team. We have completed our roster. We still have to, metaphorically speaking, finish the game.

In this lesson, we will talk about four types of ongoing, church-based care: (1) social support, (2) counseling advocate, (3) deacon care, and (4) pastoral guidance. If you are the pastor who has been running point on this situation during its crisis phase, you can relax a bit because only one of these has your name on it.

Social Support: Abuse inevitably destabilizes someone's social network. The simple question, "Who in our church do you trust enough that you would like them to intentionally walk with you during this time?" can pay exponential benefits in the weeks and months ahead. This question creates a care team.

With this list of people a victim provides, the pastor can:

1. ask each person if they would be willing to serve on a care team for an abused member;
2. if yes, update those individuals on the situation and what has been done to this point;
3. explain the team's primary functions (see below);
4. identify the member of the team who will serve as the liaison with the pastors-elders-deacons.

Send this video link to the care team members so you don't have to explain everything. The functions of a care team usually include:

- Encourage and assist the individual to take care of themselves: sleep, eating habits, spiritual disciplines, not isolating, exercise, or engaging personal interests to help them maintain endurance.
- Provide an emotional outlet. If all conversations about their life context are action-oriented, the individual can feel like a problem to be solved (a burden) more than a person to be heard. The care team can "just listen," directing needed questions to the appropriate person: counselor or pastor.
- Including the individual in their life rhythms can alleviate large spaces of empty time.
- Support the individual through prayer.
- Assist with or communicate service needs to the church's deacons.
- Communicate guidance needs to the pastor overseeing the care team; especially if the victim is female, a care team prevents the church's care from being predominantly male.

In the follow up section at the end of this lesson, an article is included on how to "care for the care team," which is an often overlooked part of the process.

HEAR FROM THE EXPERTS

 Question for Subject Area Experts: What are best, most replicable practices that you have seen churches do to care for a victim of abuse after necessary reporting or decision about pressing charges? What simple things, though they are easy to overlook, tend to be most meaningful and have the biggest impact?

 Answers from Subject Area Experts: Watch the experts' responses at churchcares.com, under the Video Training section, in the video entitled: *Lesson 9 – Pastoral Care After Reporting: Reporting Is Not a Ministerial Hand Off.*

Rachael Denhollandar: When you are walking through abuse with a survivor, it's helpful to remember that what is only a tiny part of your overall ministry, is consuming their daily life. Their life revolves around reliving terrible memories and fears of whether they are going to be safe. Life is on hold waiting to know about investigations and court dates and motions and appearances. A phone call from the investigator or prosecutor can send everything into a tailspin at any time. The daily demands of life can be very difficult.

The most important thing you can do for a survivor is let them know that what they are suffering matters to you, and it matters to God. This takes intentional, practical steps. Strategize with other church leaders to discuss questions like, who is going to check in with the survivor this week to find out about court dates and motions, to hear what things can be prayed for, and if there are court appearances someone from church can attend to offer support? Who can the survivor call if there is a crisis or immediate help needed?

Think through practical needs. You can't carry all the load yourself, so who do you need to connect the survivor to? Making sure they get put on a mealtrain in those early weeks or during a court date, having a system for letting the members know about specific needs and requesting help, and making sure the church body is kept up to date so they can pray and offer support, are all critical.

Consider whether there are organizations outside the church that you can connect them with too, like a Child Advocacy Center, a support group for wives leaving abusive husbands, or community programs to help with practical provisions like food and more permanent housing.

As you do, remember that the survivor has been given no choices, and no voice in what happened to them, so be sure to ask first what they are comfortable having shared with the congregation.

Most importantly, continue to speak the truth about what they are suffering. "This was evil, and God hates it." "I am so sorry, this was not your fault." "We are praying for God's justice to be shown on earth, because He sees and hates this too."

And don't be afraid to grieve with them. What they have been through, and are going through, is grief worthy, and they will need help seeing and holding onto the truth. As the shepherd of souls, you have the beautiful privilege of ministering very personally to their suffering.

Mika Edmondson: The book of Job provides some wonderful wisdom about how to walk alongside survivors as they mourn the devastation of abuse. Although Job's friends are eventually exposed as unreliable counselors, they started out well. Job 2:11 says, "Now when Job's three friends heard of all this evil that had come upon him, they came each from his own place, Eliphaz the Temanite, Bildad the Shuhite, and Zophar the Naamathite. They made an appointment together to come to show him sympathy and comfort him" (ESV). Job's friends began by putting Job's suffering on their calendar, coming together to show him compassion.

Once a survivor has reported their abuse, it's important that leadership meet together to plan how to continue care. It's helpful to devise and maintain a schedule of regular check-ins. The most important thing is helping the survivor know they are not alone. Putting the survivor's name on a list with assigned persons is crucial because of the awful impact of failing to check in. Isolation is one of the terrible dynamics of abuse. Failing to check-in may unwittingly communicate a lack of care. Check-ins may take the form of phone calls and/or visits depending on what make the survivor most comfortable. Meeting together is crucial to providing the best care possible for a survivor. None of us alone is wise. Multiple perspectives about how best to provide care can help catch potential blind spots in the care provided.

"And when they saw him from a distance, they did not recognize him. And they raised their voices and wept, and they tore their robes and sprinkled dust on their heads toward heaven" (Job 2:12 ESV). Next Job's friends provided a ministry of tears. Their emotional response matched Job's pain. With each new stage of responding to abuse, survivors find themselves encountering new levels of pain.

Leaders do well to grieve with an intensity befitting each new situation. Survivors need to know that they are seen and cared for. Even before Job heard the words of his friends, he heard the weeping of his friends. He knew he was seen and cared for. Pastors sometimes prioritize the strength of self-composure over the strength of love and compassion. However, the strength of love is what is called for during times of pain and grief. Jesus' own weeping at the tomb of Lazarus reveals the effectiveness of the ministry of tears. Job's friends also demonstrated a culturally appropriate show of compassion and solidarity with him. In our twenty-first century Western context, this display of dust-flinging, robe-tearing grief may seem over-the-top. However, in the Ancient Near East anything less would have seemed cold, half-hearted, or standoffish. It's vital to be sure to show care in the way others will receive it. If in the survivor's cultural context food communicates care, bring the person's favorite food dishes. You may simply say, "I'd like to do something special for you. What sorts of things would show you that someone cares?" Or "How can I make your day better?"

Finally Job 2:13 says, "And they sat with him on the ground seven days and seven nights, and no one spoke a word to him, for they saw that his suffering was very great" (ESV). Alongside the ministry of tears, Job's friends also had a ministry of ears. They took a posture of humility, alongside Job, and waited for him to speak before they ever uttered a word. It's key that leaders do lots of listening when walking with survivors. Set up sessions in which as a leader you simply ask, "What's this been like for you" or "How are you experiencing this today?" Listen patiently and non-defensively without offering any advice until your friend asks for advice. This communicates that the survivor has important wisdom and an important voice which needs to be heard.

Counseling Advocate: A counseling advocate is a *peer-based* relationship, a friend, mentor, encourager, etc., who serves as a *periodic guest* in counseling, meaning they don't come to every session. Their role is to provide *support and reinforcement* while that individual is in counseling and serve as a long-term *encouragement and accountability after counseling concludes.*

Not every counselor will be open to this possibility. *Not every victim of abuse* will want an advocate in their counseling. But when it is possible, advocates are an excellent way to bring greater continuity between the advisement being received in counseling and the ministry efforts of a local church.

In the follow up resource section, a link to a brief training for a counseling advocate is provided.

HEAR FROM THE EXPERTS

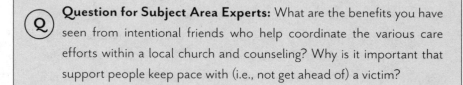

Question for Subject Area Experts: What are the benefits you have seen from intentional friends who help coordinate the various care efforts within a local church and counseling? Why is it important that support people keep pace with (i.e., not get ahead of) a victim?

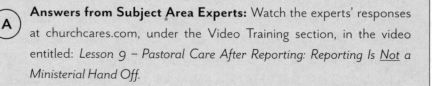

Answers from Subject Area Experts: Watch the experts' responses at churchcares.com, under the Video Training section, in the video entitled: *Lesson 9 – Pastoral Care After Reporting: Reporting Is Not a Ministerial Hand Off.*

Darby Strickland: I think it helpful to be reminded of the the isolating plight of the oppressed, the author of Ecclesiastes captures it well, "Again I saw all the oppressions that are done under the sun. And behold, the tears of the oppressed, and they had no one to comfort them! On the side of their oppressors there was power, and there was no one to comfort them" (Eccles. 4:1 ESV).

Intentional relationships lift isolation and provide the oppressed comfort and hope. I have counseled many victims of abuse, and when the body of Christ comes around them in a supportive way—I see hearts and souls beautifully restored. The damage to victims is significant; the wounds they carry are deep. Healing takes time and needs tending to. Friends who listen and help, remind them that they are not alone. They are invaluable to this process, as their presence restores hope.

Abuse effects nearly everything, having people pray with victims, help them negotiate their choices, listen to their overburdened heart, provide practical resources like babysitting or home maintenance, or even offer to go to counseling or court—says you are not alone. We are here. We see the cost and we are willing to help you bear it.

It is important that these relationships are not just about the abuse, there is more to the sufferer than what happened to them. Drawing out the other areas of their life, like their love of music, or a favorite hobby, is also a sweet gift, and ministers to their whole person.

Remember that healing and restoration unfolds at a human pace—respect that, victims do not need someone else telling them what to do, their abuser did that. It will likely take time for them to sort out what to do. It is redemptive to restore their own ability to make decisions. Intentional friends who are informed about abuse and trauma foster that. They can also keep more frequent contact making church care more organic and personal.

It is also important to point out, that statistically speaking our churches are filled with victims of abuse. Delegating and training others to enter in along with you is important, so that you and your ministry leaders are not overburdened. When a church handles one case well, the other victims watching from the sidelines will start to come forward—so it is imperative to duplicate and train.

Rachael Denhollander: Caring for someone who is healing from abuse, leaving an abusive situation, or engaged in the court process, is no small task. The physical and spiritual needs can feel overwhelming, and pastors are already exhausted and faced with an unending workload.

Having friends and church members who can step up to help cover both the physical and spiritual needs of the survivor and their family, is invaluable. Practical things like childcare during a meeting with investigators, or just so the parent can have a few hours to recuperate and recharge, are invaluable. Someone who can help with transporting kids or after-school care when a single parent can't do it all, can help ensure an abusive spouse doesn't reenter the picture because there's nowhere else for the child to go. Freezer meals that can be pulled out after a day unexpectedly filled with phone calls from investigators can bring sweet relief to an exhausted parent or spouse.

Church members can help fill these practical needs and, in doing so, communicate to the survivor, perhaps for the first time ever, that they matter and have value.

Church members who are faithfully praying for and walking alongside the survivor are also a vital ministry of mercy. Pastors can help facilitate this by making sure the congregation is kept up to date on what's happening, in a way that the survivor desires.

It is important to remember, though, that what the survivor has been through is also intensely private, and very raw. Discuss with the survivor what is going to be most helpful to them, and how best to communicate it to those who can help. Sharing more information than the survivor is ready to share, even when done with the best motives, takes away their voice and can feel very violating.

Intentional friendships are vital parts of walking alongside a survivor, but always within the framework of where the survivor is at in their healing and ability to share. For any church member who will be walking alongside a survivor, it is helpful for them to understand basic aspects of abuse, such as the damage that has been done and what sorts of things may or may not be helpful for survivors to hear. Resources that your members can utilize to be better prepared to minister to survivors, are valuable tools to have at your disposal.

Deacon Care: If you think about Acts 6, it is almost as if God created an entire role in the church for situations like we've been talking about. The early church pastors were overwhelmed trying to care for a group of people in family crisis—widows—so God raised up deacons.

Think about the kind of situations that cause an abused woman to return to her abuser: the garage door opener breaks, she doesn't know how to fix it, and doesn't have the money *so she calls him*; both her children have an event on the same day and she can't be in two places at the same time *so she calls him*; or while doing all the work in a single adult household, she cannot manage to get the yard mowed, *so she calls him*.

What is the fallout of these decisions? She goes back into his relational debt. They have an argument. He claims he was just doing what she asked and that she was trying to set him up. The pastor or care team get lots of long, emotion-laden phone calls and begin to think, "We thought you felt unsafe with him?"

A deacon who can fix a washing machine, take a kid to a baseball game, or mow a yard can prevent all of this. At the same time, the deacon's wife can spend time with the victim and further establish a sense of care and presence from the church. No advanced training is needed for these roles of inestimable value.

MINISTRY REFLECTION

Ask your deacon team to invite several women in the church who have lived through abusive marriages to come to their next meeting. Let the topic of conversation be, "How can deacon ministry best serve families navigating separation because of abuse?" What do you think would come from that conversation?

_____

_____

_____

_____

_____

Pastoral Guidance: With those other roles off your plate and an experienced abuse counselor involved, you might be asking, "What's left for me to do?" There are still several guidance roles that uniquely belong to ministry leaders.

- *Prayer*—The victim needs prayer; not just from-a-distance prayer, but in-person prayer.
- *Shepherd Through Suffering*—The aftermath of abuse is a time when doing the "right" or "wise" thing doesn't have always have immediate pleasant outcomes. Discouragement, cynicism, and confusion are common struggles that need the shepherding care of a ministry leader.
- *Wrestle Through Difficult Moral Decisions*—Abuse creates a plethora of moral dilemmas, situations where none of the options available seem "good." As you provide guidance, make sure the voice for decision-making remains with the victim and they do not place you in the position of being the "benevolent decision maker," the role that their spouse used to be in and you become the rescuer. Help them recover their own voice.
- *Coordinate Care*—The deacons and care team need a touch point for questions that arise for them.
- *Oversee Church Discipline*—If the abuser is a church member, then in the post-legal-report phase there will still be a significant amount of time and energy being poured into church discipline.

HEAR FROM THE EXPERTS

Question for Subject Area Experts: If you could give one word of instruction or encouragement to pastors and ministry leaders about the post-legal-report phase of care, what would you want them to know? This phase is often long and tedious; how would you recommend pastors seek support or guidance for this extended phase of care?

Answers from Subject Area Experts: Watch the experts' responses at churchcares.com, under the Video Training section, in the video entitled: *Lesson 9 – Pastoral Care After Reporting: Reporting Is Not a Ministerial Hand Off.*

Samantha Kilpatrick: In my legal work with abuse survivors, it is sad to report, but oftentimes, the church leaders avoid the survivor because they don't want to appear to take sides or they just feel awkward and don't know what to say. This is not a time to avoid, but rather a time to engage. As things progress in the criminal phase, check in with the victim. If a hearing is coming up—offer to go to court and sit on the "victim's side."

When I was a prosecutor, I was astonished by the church members who came to court for the perpetrator and the victim would sit all alone—it saddened me to see the message this sent to the victim, the judge, police, and the community about faith and the church. In those times, I wanted to pull the church members aside so they could read the police reports, hear the frantic 911 calls, and see the graphic photos, and maybe they would see the truth about what was really going on.

Rachael Denhollander: As you care for survivors and their families, be encouraged. While the ability to do great damage is there, it is equally true that you have the ability to do incredible good. Christ said we will be known as Christians by our love, and the ability you have to demonstrate Christlike love by ministering to the spiritual and practical needs of a survivor, may be the first time they have ever seen the love of Christ put on flesh.

Leslie Vernick: Once you get your team in place and the crisis is over, don't forget them. You may have moved on to the next crisis or church responsibility. You've wisely handed them off to a counselor, a lawyer, a prosecutor, or discipler or mentor in your church, but your parishioner still is encouraged to know that you still think about them and pray for them.

One practice you might find useful is putting them on your calendar once a month or every six weeks. When their name pops up, send a card or an e-mail letting them know that you're thinking about them. Or make a point to stop them at church, give them a hug and ask them to call you or e-mail you with an update or how you can pray for them this next week.

Even though your congregant may be well cared for by the team, he or she still needs a pastor. They don't want to feel like they've been forgotten or shoved aside. Letting them know in small ways that they are loved and important reminds them of their value both to the family of God and to God Himself.

Darby Strickland: Being abused is a devastating trauma that distorts how people see God and how they think God sees them. Victims carry with them stubborn lies that they are abandoned, unlovable, and disgraced. Never tire of encouraging victims with life-giving biblical truths, what happened to them grieves God, their suffering and wounds matter to Him and to you. You might grow weary of saying the same things again and again but remember, Scripture, itself is highly repetitive, it tells us again and again how deep and personal God's love is for us. Imitate Him, repeat His beautiful truths until they fully penetrate the wounded heart.

Chris Moles: Abuse is an "all hands on deck" issue. Long-term discipleship is a community project, so it's important to gather a strong team in regards to after-care discipleship. I can't overstate teams enough as multiple eyes on the prize provides accountability, direction, purpose, and guards against potential blind spots.

Thank you for caring enough to persevere in this area of ministry. It is hard. You are weary. Answers are not clear. Opinions about how things should be handled will vary. But it is worth it, because there is a soul looking to your church to be God's agent of refuge. Thank you for being committed to doing this well.

KEY POINTS OF THIS LESSON

- Involving legal authorities is necessary but not sufficient to fulfill a church's ministry responsibilities.
- A church must think through the resources of its entire church body, not just its paid staff.
- Even when there is disagreement about how an abuse case should be handled and it causes conflict, it is worth the effort because this person/family needs God's people on their journey.

FOLLOW UP RESOURCES

- Video Training & PDF Notes: "Becoming a Counseling Advocate" by Brad Hambrick; http://bradhambrick.com/advocate/

- Article: "Caring for the Care Team in a Crisis Situation" by Brad Hambrick; http://bradhambrick.com/careteam/

- Article: "How to Care for Abuse Survivors in Your Congregation" by Krispin Mayfield; https://www.christianitytoday.com/pastors/2017/november-web-exclusives/how-to-care-for-abuse-survivors-in-your-congregation.html

Pastoral Care and Correction for an Abuser

As we began to discuss in Lesson 4, a church does not get to choose a "client" or work exclusively from the perspective of one individual. That is the approach of mental health professionals. It has advantages for which we should be grateful. However, the church has a calling to care for all of its members. This means that we also need to be wise and skilled in how we care for someone who has a history of being abusive.

MINISTRY REFLECTION

Reflect again on the differences that emerge when a counselor can focus (and is actually is ethically required to) on one individual at a time, while a pastor is called to care not only for individuals, but for a congregation as a whole? What advantages and disadvantages emerge from each approach?

_____

_____

_____

_____

_____

One of the first things you need to know is that *abuse is private.* When you attempt to minister to someone who has been abusive, it will feel like an invasion of privacy to them. This accounts for much of the resistance you are likely to experience.

A second thing you need to know is that abusers are *used to being in control.* The demeanor they show when they are in control changes dramatically when their sense of control is threatened.

In the early phases of pastoral care, it doesn't matter whether the abusive actions were intentional or instinctual. Until an abusive individual acknowledges *what* they've done (i.e., actions and effects), it is of little pastoral value to focus on *why* they did it (i.e., intent or motive). *Though abusers may not "intend" to harm, this does not make their actions less destructive or less dangerous.*

HEAR FROM THE EXPERTS

Question for Subject Area Experts: What are common ways oppressors manipulate the process? Oppressors often truly believe they are victims; how might we be vulnerable to buying into their perspective? Is abuse necessarily indicative of mental illness or being a psychopath? How should the mental-relational health of someone who has been abusive be vetted?

Answers from Subject Area Experts: Watch the experts' responses at churchcares.com, under the Video Training section, in the video entitled: *Lesson 10 – Pastoral Care and Correction for an Abuser.*

Chris Moles: Abusers are master manipulators, in much the same way that a magician uses misdirection to create an illusion or a clever deception, an abuser will attempt to place our focus on any number of secondary issues. That is why it is important that we remain focused in our understanding and approaches. This is easier said than done as the culture at large and the church have propagated myths regarding abuse that overwhelmingly benefit the abuser. Here are the most prominent myths I've encountered in the church along with my critique:

1. It's an anger problem. The rationale goes that abuse is caused by anger or anger cues. And therefore we must address those in order to see change. The problem is that abuse is not caused by anger. In fact, more than likely, anger is a tactic used by the abuser to get their way. If we only address his anger, we run the risk of creating polite abusers who commit respectable sins. And if we only address his anger cues, more than likely that will target the victim who he claims is creating the anger in the first place.

2. It's a marriage problem. While abuse often occurs in the context of marriage, that doesn't mean that it's a mutual issue. The old phrase that we hear is that, "It takes two to tango." But in dancing and relationships, it only takes one partner to mess things up. Just because it occurs in the context of marriage doesn't mean it's a mutual issue. In fact, it requires one person alone to commit acts of abuse.

3. It's the wife's problem. The rationale goes that the abuse is the result of an unsubmissive wife. And the recourse of the church is to teach biblical submission and a theology of suffering. I love biblical submission. I love a theology of suffering. But submission without the nuance of biblical headship and servant leadership is dangerous. And a theology of suffering without the theology of oppression is deadly.

4. It's a pathological problem. The rationale goes that an outside force must be causing the abuser to behave this way. Let me be clear: there's no pathological connection to domestic violence. There's no outside force that causes someone to target their victim. Substances, environment, and genetics may contribute to who we are, but abuse is a choice.

5. It's a criminal justice problem and the church's only recourse is to report. However, reporting only alleviates us of the punitive response. God graciously gave us in Romans 13 the reality that the government wields the sword but as Christians we bear the weight of the cross. Reporting doesn't alleviate our responsibility to comfort the victim or confront the perpetrator.

In reality, what we're really dealing with is a heart problem. Abuse begins in the heart of the oppressor. Therefore, the gospel is his only real hope. The most effective means of reducing abuse is to address the heart of the oppressor.

Diane Langberg: Abuse involves three components: the deception of self, the deception of others, and the coercion of others. First the abuser is self-deceived. Abuse requires deadening one's ability to discern good and evil. Truth and lies become confused or even reversed. Self-deception works in concert with temptation so we can convince ourselves of the rightness of actions that are in fact wrong. We use deception to say that external circumstances justify reactions—a classic example is domestic violence. I hit her because she . . . Self-deception functions as a narcotic, numbing us to the damage and danger of our choices. If we engage in such self-delusion long enough we will, over time, lose our taste for the good *and* our power to loathe evil. We silence the voice of God and our response of holy fear to that voice. The problem of course is that sin *will* hurt us; it will lead to death for us and others. As deception becomes a way of life, evil can be easily practiced by an increasingly dead soul that then becomes presumptuous, planning and actively participating in evil.

Having deceived ourselves, it is not hard to deceive others. We use our status, our knowledge, our personality or skills—to cover who we *are* and to present ourselves as being *for* others rather than as a user of others. A brilliant preacher cannot possibly be an abuser. A charismatic businessman who gives generously cannot possibly be hurting his children. An outstanding coach cannot possibly abuse boys. Many people, especially those with a vested interest in the abuser, allow themselves to be deceived by the abuser because they do not want to face the disrupting, troubling truth about someone they assumed was good. In fact, they are not good; they are a prowling wolf. These deceptions occur in Christian homes, churches, and institutions. Once this has happened, it is not hard to coerce a vulnerable person or a self-protective institution into deception about the abuser. The capacity for deception in all of us is why independent investigations are crucial to finding truth. And for the record, across studies the rates of false accusations runs between 3 and 9 percent.

The exposure of abuse is an invitation—a sweet invitation—to the abuser to step into the light. When deception has been so practiced in a life, exposure will first result in denial and more lies. Someone who has been abusing has lost the capacity to tell the truth to him/herself. Healing is only possible when the light shines relentlessly in the darkness until the offender falls down before our crucified God knowing that it is against that wounded Savior that he/she has sinned. That abuser demands *nothing* from any human, no position, no restoration—*including forgiveness*—acknowledging their inability to live in truth and knowing better than any they are not to be trusted and the choices behind their actions are theirs and theirs alone. As Jesus said, "What comes out of a person comes from that person and that person alone."

Any beneficial care for abusers begins with their **acknowledgement of the nature, extent, and impact of their abusive behavior**. Without this acknowledgement, working on other areas of personal growth (ways of being "nicer" or a more engaged parent) will, at best, create a façade of change. Resistance to acknowledging their abusive behavior reveals (a) this person is not repentant, and (b) this person is not safe to be back in the home.

There are two approaches recommended to gain acknowledgement. First, *focus on the clearest examples of abuse*. Self-awareness and acknowledgement typically develop from the greater to the lesser. Think in terms of a 1 to 10 scale. If the abuser's worst actions were a "9," those actions will have to be owned before they will acknowledge a "7." Once you get to a "6" or "5" event, they will likely want to treat these as "not that bad."

The objective is to help them realize that when their average or "normal" conflict response level registers as a "5 or 6," this is a healthy person's *worst* conflict response. They are forcing their family to be perpetually bracing for an unsafe response and tolerate an elevated conflict environment as their "normal."

A second approach is called *rolling with resistance*; a style of communication developed in working with individuals who are resistant to change. In the follow up resource section, an introductory tutorial on rolling with resistance is included. The basic idea is this: if you are addressing someone who lacks the motivation to change, then the *initial goal* (i.e., the first step towards the *ultimate goal*) should be on raising the level of motivation and commitment to change rather than offering solutions to the problem.

The abusive individual is going through an emotionally stressful time. *But they are not the victim of their own actions.* We can be empathetic without letting up on expectations. If past abuse, addiction, or mental health concerns contribute to their abuse, pursuing the needed care should be a requirement of the church discipline, and a release of information document should be signed so pastors can speak with whatever caregivers are involved.

HEAR FROM THE EXPERTS

(Q) Question for Subject Area Experts: What are other key strategies for cultivating self-awareness and acknowledgement within abusers regarding their abusive behavior? How can we help an individual see the underlying sense of entitlement that drives the abuse? How do we talk about the role of past abuse, addiction, or mental health concerns without these becoming excuses for the abusive behavior?

(A) Answers from Subject Area Experts: Watch the experts' responses at churchcares.com, under the Video Training section, in the video entitled: *Lesson 10 – Pastoral Care and Correction for an Abuser.*

Leslie Vernick: It's been my experience that abusive individuals are more self-aware than we give them credit for. It's not that they're unaware that their behavior has crossed the line of what's acceptable or legal, the problem is that they justify it. They have a million reasons why they are not responsible.

They are expert blame-shifters, liars, minimizers, and excuse makers. This is hard for us as Christian people helpers to see this. We want to believe that they are like us. That they didn't mean it or that their conscience is pricked as ours is and that they feel bad for hurting someone as we do. But it isn't and they don't. Instead they feel entitled.

Now don't get me wrong, you may see an abuser feeling bad but not about hurting someone.

Listen closely. When you see or hear them feeling bad it's because they were caught, and now they are experiencing a negative consequence, loss of job, legal problems, marital separation, or church discipline.

It's this entitlement thinking that must be identified and changed if we're going to ever see a subsequent behavior change that sticks long term.

So how can we, as people helpers, help someone see their entitled thinking?

1. *Set limits and boundaries and expectations early on within your own relationship.* The abuser will feel entitled to violate them. When they do, ask good questions like, "Why are you the exception to the rule, I've asked you not to text me or call me at home and yet you continue to do so?"

2. *Never accept an excuse for abusive behavior.* "So your husband cheated on you. So your wife refuses to engage sexually as often as you want. So your stepdaughter dressed provocatively. So you were abused as a child. So you are diagnosed bipolar or an alcoholic." These facts may be true, however; they don't entitle someone to abuse others. Once we start accepting excuses for abuse, all hope for the abuser taking personal responsibility will end. Personal responsibility may start with submitting to treatment for mental illness or addiction problems, but never excuse abuse. There are plenty of mentally ill people who do not abuse others.

3. *Actions always speak louder than words.* Promises are meaningless; only consistent actions over time show real change. Promises to stop drinking, go to counseling, or take medication are worthless. Don't get excited about promises. You want to see change.

4. *Communicate clearly your expectations.* "I want you to come to appointment on time," or "I want you to stop interrupting me." And watch how they respond.

5. *Test change in the here and now.* If they don't show movement in the here and now, by listening to your feedback and correction, there is no change happening at home. They are still entitled.

Chris Moles: Luke 6:45 tell us, "A good man brings good things out of the good stored up in his heart, and an evil man brings evil things out of the evil stored up in his heart. For the mouth speaks what the heart is full of."

I want to be as concrete and up-front with people as possible. Abuse is caused by abusers, not substances, anger, immodesty, family history. Abuse is a choice that the offender has made and these behaviors are not random; they flow from his inner person.

So through the initial stages of intervention I expect to uncover the following:

1. A list of abusive behavior consistent with the power and control wheel through dialogue with the abuser, as well as input from the victim.

2. A corresponding list of effects or impact of the abusive behavior. I ask questions regarding consequences or effects to the abuse, such as "Was your partner afraid of you? Was anyone physically hurt? Has your partner experienced depression or anxiety?"

3. I want to create a corresponding list of motivations from which these actions flow. I asked "what-based" questions in response to the known abuse to highlight motivates. Questions like, "What did you want to see happen when you punched a hole in the wall?" or "What benefits did you experience by screaming profanity at your partner?"

4. I want to look at any core beliefs or values that are now clear based on numbers 1–3.

The fruit of domestic abuse indicates the roots of pride, entitlement, and control. Saying hard things in safe places allows us to honestly assess the problem and offer correct, biblical solutions. Once we have identified the sinful abusive behavior in his life we look into the motives and beliefs associated with them. These are far more difficult to identify at first but we will not be prepared to call him to repentance without them.

James 4 tells us, "What causes fights and quarrels among you? Don't they come from your desires that battle within you? You desire but do not have, so you kill. You covet but you cannot get what you want, so you quarrel and fight."

As is the case with a lot of discipleship, properly highlighting sinful behavior and motivation is only the beginning as we then call the sinner to repentance by abandoning both the abusive behavior as well as the desires and embracing new godly motivations and behavior. This stage must be just as concrete if we are to evaluate change and will include the following:

1. Specifics statements of repentance
2. New biblically informed and godly motivation
3. An after-care plan of discipleship consistent with progressive sanctification

---

This raises the question: How can we tell if an abuser is changing in meaningful ways? What are the key qualities that should serve as markers to show us change is happening? We will discuss four.

Humility: How do you know when you are talking to a humble person? They ask good questions and listen. When we don't listen well, we are trapped in our own way of interpreting life. Bad listeners are by definition self-centered. Blame-shifting will stop as humility emerges.

Patience: When a humble person hears the pain their abuse has caused, they do not rush or demand a gracious response. Until an abusive person can say, "I created a destructive environment in our marriage for years. You are learning to see me as a safe person. It is hard for me to be patient, but it is harder for you to trust. I am willing to accept that and focus on needed changes in my life," they are not patient.

Accountability: Why does most abuse happen in homes? In a word, privacy. *Privacy kills change and fuels sin. Transparency kills sin and fuels change.* An abusive person desiring to change will be honest with at least three types of people: (1) a pastor or elder, (2) a counselor with experienced with abuse, and (3) members of the church discipline restoration team.

MINISTRY REFLECTION

Consider the connection between humility, patience, and accountability. Ask yourself the question, "How would someone prone to being abusive ever resist this temptation or change if they were not humble enough to be patient with those they hurt and invite others to hold them accountable?"

_____

_____

_____

_____

_____

Robust Repentance: The abusive individual must not construe repentance as "groveling." Complying with church discipline is not "going the extra mile." Accepting the consequences of one's sin is not being a martyr. To portray these evidences of genuine change as groveling is to recast repentance into the old self-centered narrative and is *a major red flag for the recurrence of abuse.*

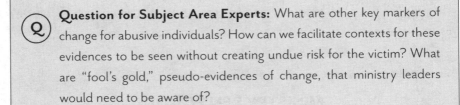

HEAR FROM THE EXPERTS

Q **Question for Subject Area Experts:** What are other key markers of change for abusive individuals? How can we facilitate contexts for these evidences to be seen without creating undue risk for the victim? What are "fool's gold," pseudo-evidences of change, that ministry leaders would need to be aware of?

A **Answers from Subject Area Experts:** Watch the experts' responses at churchcares.com, under the Video Training section, in the video entitled: *Lesson 10 – Pastoral Care and Correction for an Abuser.*

Darby Strickland: When an oppressor is repentant, we will see an entirely different fruit in their lives. We must be careful to not fall for displays of worldly regret which are characterized by remorse for how their sin is causing *them* suffering. We are looking for godly regret which is focused on how it offends God and brings restoration and redemption to others. Zacchaeus, the tax collector, displays this type of repentance. It begins with confession, but is also evidenced by works that stem from heart change. Zacchaeus was not only ready to give satisfaction for what he took by fraud, but shared half of his own lawful possessions with the poor.

The genuinely repentant confess comprehensive detailed past entitlements and controlling behavior without blame shifting, and acknowledge that their behavior was purposeful. Repentant people see the effects of their sin and express empathy for the wounds it caused others; they are willing to make amends and accept the consequences for their actions. They will be patient with their victims, not pressuring them or using guilt to broker forgiveness. There will be an eagerness to lay down their power and control in concrete and tender ways. The only person who will know if this is really happening is their victim—so it is critical to get their input when assessing repentance.

Samantha Kilpatrick: When I was a prosecutor in the domestic violence unit, the most frustrating part of my work was the recidivism. There are programs out there that try to teach anger management and stress management as ways to control the temper and lessen occurrences of violence. The truth of the matter is this is not about anger management or marriage issues– violence and abuse are character issues involving power and control that makes abusing another person okay, even deserved in the eyes of the offender.

You do not arrive at a violent episode or criminal charge overnight, so in thinking about change and repentance, know that it will not happen quickly—in fact—if you are seeing "quick" signs—it is most likely an act. With true repentance, you will see a person, changed in many areas but mostly as it relates to their pride, ego, and needs—putting those at the very back and doing everything asked to make things right—day by day, week by week, month by month, year by year, no matter how long it takes.

Mika Edmondson: Ephesians 4:28 reveals a helpful pattern of genuine repentance. It says "Let the thief no longer steal, but rather let him labor, doing honest work with his own hands, so that he may have something to share with anyone in need" (ESV). Though this passage is specifically dealing with the sin of theft, this same pattern of repentance can be applied to abuse. Notice the thief is called to do more than stop his behavior, but to demonstrate a sustained and costly commitment to reverse course aimed at serving vulnerable persons. True repentance from abuse would at least involve the following:

1. Immediately stop abusing this victim and all others (freely confessing the sin with godly sorrow)

2. Committing over time to try and repair the damage caused to past victims (no matter how long it takes, even if the relationship is never restored)

3. Committing to become generous to victims of abuse when they are ready to receive it, helping to reverse the effects of this kind of sin against other victims. Having "something to share with anyone in need" means deliberately seeking to become educated about the dynamics of abuse, finding various ways to advocate for victims, raising awareness about abuse, and sacrificially supporting survivors without recompense.

False repentance often looks like a commitment to one of these at the expense of others. For instance, some people temporarily stop abusive behaviors but have no sustained and costly commitment to reverse course. Others may stop a behavior but they are constantly looking for shortcuts to restoration; they are not willing to put their shoulder to the plow to make things right and serve others. Finally, some people demonstrate a form of grief and changed behavior toward one particular victim while remaining cold toward the plight of other potential victims.

We need to ask two more questions: What if the abusive individual is married and does not repent? What if the abusive individual is married and their spouse is slow or unwilling to trust their spouse's repentance?

First, if the abusive spouse does not repent, then the church should *remove them from membership, and support the abused spouse in whatever decision they need to make for their safety.*

Even if a church does not believe that continued abuse fits the abandonment clause of 1 Corinthians 7, their choice is not between one holy and one unholy option. The choice is between empowering an abuser and supporting a victim pursuing of safety. Child custody and removing financial leverage often require taking legal steps. *A victim of abuse should have the support of their church in taking the steps necessary to ensure their safety.* If questioned by the abuser or another church member on this, the response should be something like:

> "It would be hypocritical for an abusive spouse to condemn their spouse for separation while not addressing their abusive behaviors. As a church, we do not view prolonged separation or divorce as worse than refusing to change abusive behavior. Unfortunately, those were the only options the abusive spouse left to their family. In abusive situations, *we do not tell the victim what they ought to do.* We believe that is a matter of conscience and wisdom. *We do support the victims of abuse in the choices they need to make for their own safety and the safety of their children.*"

If church discipline has been done well, the actions of the abusive spouse are public enough for this type of statement to be made to church members who are concerned about the church's stance on marriage.

Second, if the abusive spouse repents and manifests evidence of change, but the abused spouse is slow to trust, the church should advocate for continued patience on the part of the formerly abusive spouse *for as long as safety arrangements are not causing greater distress for the children.* It is hypocritical to expect forgiveness and trust in a shorter amount of time than it took the abuser to come to repent—which includes the months or years before the church became aware of the abuse.

The assessment for the children's well-being should be made by an experienced child therapist. The church should position itself with the best interest of the weakest and most vulnerable at the forefront of their concern—in this case, the children.

In these questions, we face one of the realities of abuse: abuse reduces the number of ideal options and multiplies the number of choices we wish we didn't have to make. Here, again, we enter the world of the oppressed. When abuse is present, no one likes the options before them, but we can be a refuge for the oppressed and, however uncomfortable that may be, it is good and godly to be such.

KEY POINTS OF THIS LESSON

- Beneficial correction of abusers begins with their acknowledgement of nature, extent, and impact of abusive behavior.
- Four key markers of change are: humility, patience, accountability, and repentance.
- In abusive situations, we do not tell the victim what they ought to do (unless they are required by law to take a certain course of action). We do support the victims of abuse in the choices they need to make for their own safety and the safety of their children.

FOLLOW UP RESOURCES

- Article: "Manipulative Repentance: 8 Red Flag Phrases" by Brad Hambrick; http://bradhambrick.com/manipulative-repentance-8-red-flag-phrases/

- Article: "Conversations with Someone Not Ready to Change: Rolling with Resistance" by Brad Hambrick; http://bradhambrick.com/resistance/

Response to Abuse by a Church Leader

In this lesson we will be providing guidance on how to respond if a church leader is abusive *in their role as pastor or ministry leader*. This lesson provides unique guidance for situations like:

- A pastor or staff member is in some way abusive towards their direct reports or volunteers.
- A staff member or volunteer molests a child or teenager under their ministry care.
- A pastor engaged in sexual activity with a staff member or congregant.

Note: The power differential between a church leader and church member makes the consent language of "having an affair with" inaccurate in most cases. This would be like saying a therapist had an affair with a client or college professor with a student. The more accurate language is "sexualized abuse of power."

What is the main difference when an offense is by a church leader? It is intensely personal. This is our friend and colleague. What happens when things are personal? We ask *personal* rather than *procedural* questions.

MINISTRY REFLECTION

Imagine you just found out a fellow church staff member or key volunteer had been physically or sexually abusive towards a child or teenager. What is your initial response? Does it include both cognitive thoughts and emotional responses? How would these responses make a difference in how you handled this situation?

_____

_____

_____

_____

_____

We want to start by grounding our response in the same decision making system we have been outlining for the last ten lessons. Our first questions are *not*, "How could you do this? Why didn't I see it? Why didn't you tell me? What are we going to do with the fallout?" These are personal questions.

We start by asking two basic questions and with one underlying assumption:

Question One: *Did the offenses in this situation have any criminal element?* If anything in the offense was potentially criminal, these actions need to be handled according the guidance in question two. The standard is "potentially criminal" because the church is not an investigative body, it is a redemptive community.

Question Two: *Were the victims in this situation adults or minors?* If minors were harmed, then reporting to CPS is the next step. If adults were harmed, the victim has the legal right to choose when and if legal action is in their best interest. The next step for the church would be to connect the victim(s) with a counselor experienced helping victims in the area of offense to help them discern how they would like to proceed.

Both the victim(s) and counselor(s) should be informed that *the church will support whatever decision a victim makes regarding pressing relevant legal charges.* The counselor should *not* be on the church staff or a member of the church in order to prevent a bias from influencing advisements about what is best for the victim(s).

Assumption: *We do not know everything we need to know. Rarely does all the relevant information come to light when a crisis initially breaks.* Too often in crises churches take the intense emotions of remorse from the person they know well as validation of the words, "I've told you everything. I promise."

The assistance provided in the early stages of any crisis is merely triage care with the expectation that additional information will come to light, which will in turn change what the care plan should be.

HEAR FROM THE EXPERTS

Question for Subject Area Experts: What other key questions or assumptions are important for church leaders to consider when a fellow staff member or volunteer is involved in a major moral and/or criminal failure? What do you do if you do not believe the accusation? How should we be thinking biblically about protecting our local church's reputation compared to protecting the reputation of Christ?

Answers from Subject Area Experts: Watch the experts' responses at churchcares.com, under the Video Training section, in the video entitled: *Lesson 11 – Response to Abuse by a Church Leader.*

Diane Langberg: In the previous lesson we spoke about deception. It is important in this lesson as well. God says we are so deceived, slippery, and crafty that we do not even know ourselves, let alone anyone else. That means any accusation has to be considered very carefully and with great humility. When abuse is named, you find yourself confronting the possibility of the unthinkable and certainly the unwanted. Like a victim you will want to make it untrue. If the accused is a person well-known to us, we will be invested in the claim being false. After all, we have known him/her well for years so we say, "I know him; I trust him." But again, the Word of God speaks—Jesus trusted no man *because He knew* what was in him. So Jesus says of all of us, I know him but I do not trust him! As previously mentioned, the combination of the inevitable presence of deceit alongside the research showing that false allegations are 3–9 percent of abuse reports, then humility and finding an independent investigator are critical.

We must also remember that God's kingdom is the kingdom of the heart. It is not found in human institutions or organizations but in human hearts. If we begin serving the system rather than the holy God of the system, we will begin covering up toxins such as sexual abuse and domestic violence in order to "preserve" the institution—one that has already been poisoned. In doing this we are ignoring the equivalent of untreated cancer, denying or hiding symptoms so the system can continue, deceiving ourselves about the growing cancer within. No so-called Christian system is truly God's unless it is full of truth and light. To ignore, pretend, deny, or avoid dealing with alleged sin in our midst is to call him "Lord, Lord" and yet not do the things that He says. The damage to the sheep—victim, perpetrator and body of Christ—is incalculable. G. Campbell Morgan said this, "Sanctuary means having no complicity with those things that make sanctuary a necessity."

Rachael Denhollander: The two most important things to remember about abuse are that it rarely looks like you think it will look, and it's rarely the person you think it will be. Abusers are incredibly skilled manipulators who groom not only their victims, but also the community surrounding the victim, because abusers know that is key to helping them stay in power.

One of the first responses victims almost universally hear when they disclose abuse is "how is that possible because . . ." and then the person will have reasons why the accused couldn't be an abuser, or why abuse couldn't have happened that way.

What you need to understand is that the very dynamics making you question the victim's story, are usually the very dynamics that make the victim's story possible. Those are the very dynamics that gave the abuser power, and kept victims silent. And if you think it seems implausible to you to hear it, imagine the confusion and disbelief the victim has felt living it.

Victims are keenly aware of all the reasons they aren't likely to be believed, which is why, by the time a victim speaks up, an abuser has usually thoroughly groomed the community around him too, and you may be part of that.

You must take the lead in pursuing the truth and show by your words and conduct that it's what you really want, even if the survivor's story seems implausible. Bear in mind that false accusations are incredibly rare, and if you fail to heed this warning, you will not only do incredible damage to the survivor, but may in fact facilitate the abuse of others yet unharmed.

Most importantly, remember that Jesus Christ does not need your protection. The gospel of Christ doesn't ride on the shoulders of any one person or one local church. Pursuing the truth doesn't hurt Christ, but failing to pursue it will damage everything.

The assumption leads us to another question: how do we get the information we need? The answer to this question will vary based on the nature of the offense. But here are five transferable principles to help us get there:

1. If the offenses are illegal, the church will get information from the criminal investigation. Legal processes are slow. But when an offense is criminal in nature, the church must have patience to allow Romans 13 to run its course. Though a person is "innocent until proven guilty" in our culture, when credible reports of abuse are levied against a church leader, that leader should be given a leave of absence until the legal process is complete.

2. Confiscate church technology from the offender immediately. As a church, we cannot confiscate private property. But we can repossess any computer provided to a staff member and reclaim their church email account and calendar. This step prevents altering or deleting any of the information relevant to the situation. If the offense is illegal, law enforcement will also want to review these.

3. When the victims know their care comes first, victims are usually willing to share their experience. The order of operations here is essential. The victim must know that their safety and recovery comes first. Connecting the victim with a counselor, supporting any legal decision, and creating a care team all communicate that the church has the victim's needs ahead of their own (Phil. 2:3–4). When this is done, victims usually trust the church to use their information with integrity to care for the entire congregation.

4. If applicable, the church will want to hear from others in a role comparable to the known victim(s). Examples include: if the offense was against a subordinate staff member, interview the leader's other direct reports; or, if the offense occurred on a mission trip, interview others who traveled with the leader. For illegal offenses, law enforcement will do these interviews and the church should cooperate by providing all relevant information.

5. Lastly, and vetted through lenses of credibility, the church can get information from the offender. Offenders have the most information, but should be considered the least reliable source of information. By virtue of being in the role they were in for an extended period of time and hiding the events that transpired, they have proven a willingness to hide information or distort the narrative around events.

Here are several signs that the offender's answers are worth considering, though these should be vetted through a lens of credibility:

- *Their responses are corroborated by victims or another third party.*
- *They give more information to your questions than required or just a minimalist answer.*
- *They do not give less relevant, hyper-spiritualized answers.* After a major failure, Christians are prone to say things like, "I hadn't been the spouse or parent I should have been," or, "My quiet time had been non-existent for months." While these are areas of concern, they focus on things far less consequential than abusing one's role as a spiritual authority to harm others. It gives a veneer of being deeply broken but moves the focus away from the primary offense.

HEAR FROM THE EXPERTS

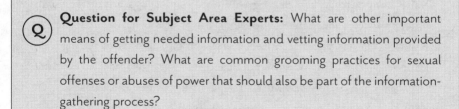

Question for Subject Area Experts: What are other important means of getting needed information and vetting information provided by the offender? What are common grooming practices for sexual offenses or abuses of power that should also be part of the information-gathering process?

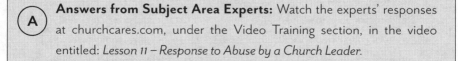

Answers from Subject Area Experts: Watch the experts' responses at churchcares.com, under the Video Training section, in the video entitled: *Lesson 11 – Response to Abuse by a Church Leader.*

Andrea Munford: Grooming can present in different ways, depending on the motive. It can be gifts, money, other items, or services. It can be time spent with someone, under the pretense of supporting them and understanding them. Grooming can be the process of building trust with a victim and others, or it can be the development of the persona they want a victim and others to see. And grooming isn't applied only to a victim; it's quite often used on parents, caretakers, other support people in a victim's life, and people in authority. It's important to keep in mind that an offender will use these grooming techniques to ingratiate themselves to those a victim may disclose to, or to someone in position to follow up on the disclosure. In doing so, the offender can create doubt in the victim and their story.

How can you vet out the information given by both parties? Start off by not judging. By not assuming that the victim has any motive to report other than they have been abused and they need help. And be mindful of the behavior of the offender. Are they answering questions, or are they just focused on the behavior of the victim and what they must be doing wrong? Do they continuously cloud the situation by referring back to what a "good person" they are, and how connected and helpful they are in the church or community?

Diane Langberg: When dealing with an offender, you are dealing with someone who is incapable of speaking truth—about himself, the victim, or others. He has habituated deceit and numbed himself to feeling pain about his actions. The more we practice deceit the more incapable we are of speaking or even recognizing truth. Again, deceit functions like a narcotic and it is ingested in order to silence guilt or empathy for others so that a deadened soul can continue its destructions.

To groom someone is to train them for a certain purpose or activity. An abuser works to bring a victim into a place they would normally reject or be horrified by, if directly asked but by doing it little by little the end goal is not recognized. It is like continually creating a mist as you walk with someone until they fall off a cliff they could not see. So offenders may come into churches and be generous, helpful with the duties, kind and gracious, wooing a vulnerable human being into a place of seeming care where an unseen wolf is waiting. When the victim cries out, everyone says the perpetrator is so nice, helpful, etc., it cannot be true when in fact such qualities were deliberately used to deceive. Such grooming is even easier when the abuser is a person with power—pastor, youth director, doctor, teacher or coach, etc., because we make character assumptions about leaders often without testing them to see if they are true.

These dynamics and a lack of understanding about abuse make the church an easy place for abusers to find victims. They say so. Training, getting help with policies and enforcing them no matter who is involved—educating leaders and members how to respond to stories of abuse, and what processes to follow so all are cared for, is vital if the body of Christ is to function as light in these dark places. When these things happen, the body is following her Head and demonstrating before a watching world that God came in the flesh and is indeed our Refuge and our Sanctuary.

Rachael Denhollander: It cannot be said enough—abusers are incredibly skilled manipulators. They can demonstrate shock, disbelief, grief, and the full range of emotions with stunning precision. They are also often skilled communicators. They know what language will disarm a pastor or church member, what language will help shift the blame, minimize their conduct, or convince people that nothing has gone wrong. Abusers can wield Scripture and theology like a weapon.

This is one of the main reasons that turning the information and investigation over to someone who is qualified to do it, is critical. Pastors are simply not trained in evidentiary law, victim-centered investigative techniques or the impact of trauma. They are not experts in understanding and identifying abusive patterns, personalities, or grooming techniques. That's okay! There are others who are. Your job is to involve those experts, and then stand back and truly let them do their job, willing to accept what they find.

Police officers are necessary for any criminal allegation, but outside private investigative agencies can also be helpful for claims that the police can't investigate, or if there is concern that the church may have mishandled warning signs or previous reports of abuse. But be very careful to only work with organizations staffed by qualified experts, with no connections to your church, who are determined to find the truth. As much as you possibly can, involve the survivor in selecting any private entities who will be investigating, so they can be as sure as possible that the truth is being sought.

The remaining question is one of circles and timing of communication. When a staff member or volunteer in your church commits a major offense there will be ripples of awareness that begin to emerge. Church leaders may not initially know the extent of the situation well enough to communicate as effectively as they would like. That is the nature of an "emerging situation." The following three circles of communication are meant to help you think through these challenges.

Circle One: *Who needs to be aware to ensure the care for any known or potential victim?* This is priority number one. Communication in this circle entails making all mandated legal reports, connecting the victim with an experienced counselor, and creating a care team. These actions cannot wait until you have the whole story.

Circle Two: *What does your congregation need to know in order to maintain trust with its leaders?* This circle involves updating the church about what is currently known and what is being done to learn more.

The best way to dispel rumors is with the truth. The best way to prevent gossip is by being forthcoming. The basic questions that need to be answered are: What happened? How did it come to light? What is currently being done? When will more information be available? Answers to these questions should be clear, concise, and avoid speculation.

The names of victims should *not* be used. As much as possible, information should be communicated in a way to limit the impact on the offender's family. Information communicated with the church-at-large, as part of church discipline, becomes "public domain" and no longer falls under pastor-parishioner privilege.

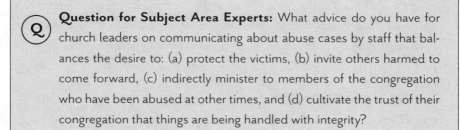

HEAR FROM THE EXPERTS

Q **Question for Subject Area Experts:** What advice do you have for church leaders on communicating about abuse cases by staff that balances the desire to: (a) protect the victims, (b) invite others harmed to come forward, (c) indirectly minister to members of the congregation who have been abused at other times, and (d) cultivate the trust of their congregation that things are being handled with integrity?

A **Answers from Subject Area Experts:** Watch the experts' responses at churchcares.com, under the Video Training section, in the video entitled: *Lesson 11 – Response to Abuse by a Church Leader.*

Karla Siu: As anyone who has been in leadership can attest, we will encounter difficult situations that will require us to call on wise counsel to discern the way forward. Allegations of abuse by church staff will require both transparency and discretion. It is not possible to provide you with **specific to-do's** that you can follow in these difficult situations given the unique and sensitive nature of each case. However, I do urge you to (1) seek *expert* counsel from outside your congregation (2) proceed with humility and a willingness to allow for *outside investigation* of **every** allegation that is brought forth—yes, even those raised against individuals or friends who we hold up as the best among us. Church leaders must both uphold and adhere to a transparent set of policies and procedures.

Even David, a man after God's own heart, needed Nathan to expose his sin because David was unwilling. We must emulate King David's attitude towards accountability in Psalm 139 where he boldly prays, "Search me, O God, and know my heart! Try me and know my thoughts! And see if there be any grievous way in me."

Likewise, we must allow others to point out our sins. If we are guilty, then allowing the light to expose our sin is foundational to our healing—both our own and the congregation's. On the other hand, if we have been falsely accused, as Christians we call upon the Lord, our strongest defender. It's in this place that our faith and leadership will be tested most, but when we run towards the light He will make plain all things that are confounded by darkness.

Rachael Denhollander: Pastors understandably can feel caught in the middle when a leader or employee is accused of abuse. How do you pursue the truth without "entertaining a charge against an elder" unless there is real evidence? One of the first steps is to have a flat church policy of always making the congregation aware of an abuse allegation. You should do this without revealing the identity of the alleged victim, but with enough facts that congregants who may have information can realize they hold a piece of the puzzle and know what to do with it. Notifying the congregation should also include some sort of instruction for who ought to be considered a potential victim and where to go if someone suspects more abuse has occurred to others in the church. This blanket policy ensures that you aren't the one weighing the credibility of an allegation or "accepting a charge," and also helps take the sting out of the process in the event you do receive a false accusation.

Mika Edmondson: As Paul offers this counsel about addressing the sins of leaders. "As for those who persist in sin, rebuke them in the presence of all, so that the rest may stand in fear. In the presence of God and of Christ Jesus and of the elect angels I charge you to keep these rules without prejudging, doing nothing from partiality" (1 Tim. 5:20–21 ESV). Here, the Scripture recognizes our common tendency to be partial toward our leaders. Abusive leaders are not immediately recognized as such. They can be charming, kind, deferential, competent, and empathetic. They help provide a sense of identity, purpose, and direction to the congregation. It can be traumatic for a church community to discipline and part ways with an abusive leader.

Rather than deal with this directly, we can easily find ourselves covering for abusive leaders, dismissing or downplaying their abusive behaviors, or skewing the facts in a way that will allow us to avoid facing realities we'd rather not deal with. Therefore Paul must charge us before God, to do the right thing when it comes to the hard task of disciplining an abusive leader. These steps can help:

1. Bring in an independent investigator to help investigate and confirm the facts of alleged abuse. Sometimes congregations need help remaining impartial toward people they love so deeply and think they know so well. People will also need to know that the deck is not stacked on behalf of the leader.

2. Remove the accused leader from serving in their position (and out of any place where he/she has access to children or contact with the victim) until after the investigation has been fully conducted. This is crucial in order to maintain impartiality and to protect the congregation. Temporarily stepping down during an investigation can be established as a condition upon hiring a leader.

3. Communicate with the congregation verbally and in writing informing them of the name of the abusive leader and the basic allegation/s. This should be done specifically in consultation with law-enforcement and knowledgeable experts. Ineffective communication could potentially harm the victim as well as the investigation. Although helpful communication can be tricky, leaders may need to inform the congregation of basic facts in order to encourage any additional victims to come forward.

4. Give the congregation something to do. Be sure to encourage them to mourn with those who mourn, to pray that God's justice will be established, God's truth will be revealed, that sin and injuries will be healed, that peace, purity, and unity will be granted to the congregation through this.

5. A single accusation is sufficient to warrant an investigation of a leader.

6. If the leader is found to be guilty, discipline must be public, and impartial because they hold a public office. This is vital for the protection of the congregation.

Circle Three: *What does your community need to know in order to view the church as an institution of integrity?* Circle three is a response to when an offense becomes public outside the church. The world around us needs to hear of churches handling abuse cases well. If not, this will (and should) greatly hamper our gospel witness.

For the sake of the victims, we do not increase the awareness of their suffering. Unfortunately, there will be ample opportunity for churches to display good responses to abuse. As we communicate about cases that become public that we are handling them according to the principles of this curriculum, the church can again become the place where the most vulnerable in our communities seek refuge. May God let it be so!

KEY POINTS OF THIS LESSON

- Unless you are highly intentional, you will not handle an offense by a staff member or volunteer the way you do another church member.

- When a crisis breaks, you should operate on the assumption that all relevant information is not known regardless of how much the offender tells you otherwise.

- The priorities that guide communication are: (1) the safety and well-being of the victim, (2) the appropriate awareness of the covenant family, (3) the reputation of the body of Christ in the community as a place that handles abuse well.

FOLLOW UP RESOURCES

- "Manipulative Repentance: 8 Red Flag Phrases" by Brad Hambrick; http://bradhambrick.com/manipulative-repentance -8-red-flag-phrases/

Seven Next Steps after this Training

Thank you for your diligence to complete this study. You have many ministry responsibilities. We appreciate the investment of time you have given to ensure your church is a context of excellent care for those who have experienced various forms of abuse.

In this final lesson, we want to help you be the catalyst to ensure key leaders in your church receive the pieces of this training that are most pertinent to their ministry. We also want to suggest things you can do in the coming months to solidify the lasting impact of this training on how you do ministry.

With that in mind, here are seven steps to consider as your conclude this training:

Step One: *Talk with an Abuse Victim*—Without this conversation, many of the things we've discussed may feel theoretical. There may be nothing you can do to solidify what you've learned like having a conversation with a victim who needed a ministry leader equipped in these ways.

A simple way to cultivate this conversation would be: print a copy of this packet, give it to a member of your church who experienced abuse, ask them to watch the training series, and then invite them to share their thoughts.

For them, it may be the first time they felt like their experience was understood by a church. For you, it will be a conversation that puts a face, name, and story to the principles and practices we've covered.

Step Two: *Talk with an Attorney about Your State's Laws*—You may have an attorney in your congregation who would do this for free. Even if not, it will be money well spent. Go to Appendix A, highlight the statutes for your state, and ask them to translate the legal jargon into normal English. If their first attempt to translate is unclear, ask them to try again. Don't leave until you can articulate your state's laws in everyday language.

Before this meeting, create a list of questions. Having case examples, perhaps from your conversation with a victim, will help you gain a better understanding of the laws. If you have a hard time creating questions and case examples, skip to step three and have that conversation first.

Step Three: *Talk with a Social Worker*—Perhaps have a lunch conversation or invite a social worker to do a Q&A with your church staff. Here are several questions that should be part of the conversation:

- What are the best resources in our community for victims of abuse?
- What are the most common mistakes you've seen churches make in handling abuse?
- What are the best ways you've seen churches be an asset in abuse or neglect cases?
- Can you give us an anonymous abuse case study that we could think through together?
- If we have a question about an abuse case, who would consult with us?

If you send these questions in advance, you are likely to get a written list of qualified counselors and community resources. Show yourself to be a church that genuinely cares about handling abuse cases well and the quality of consultation you will get on future abuse cases will increase.

MINISTRY REFLECTION

What questions would you want to ask a social worker after listening to this series?

_____

_____

_____

_____

_____

Step Four: _Review Key Church Policies_—As a result of going through this study, you will read your existing policies differently. You may see gaps that need to be filled. Or, you may merely understand better why some of the "best practice" language you adopted from another church is worded the way that it is.

Here are several key policies you need to review, both written policy and execution review:

- What is the background check policy for all church staff and volunteers? Is it being consistently put into practice?
- Is this **churchcares.com** training a requirement for all staff at your church?
- Do you have adequate policies for your children ministry to ensure the safety of children? When was the last time you did a quality control review of how these are being implemented?
- Do you know how to create and effectively oversee a care team?
- Do you have a policy to ensure proper reporting in cases of sexual abuse against a minor by a staff member or church volunteer?

- Do you have a policy on the attendance and accountability expectations of a registered sex offender who wants to attend or become a member of your church?
- Do you contact the prior church of those seeking to join your membership, asking questions about their character, causes for concern, reasons for leaving?

While the awareness that these reviews need to occur is fresh, go ahead and send an email to each person who would oversee the relevant area of ministry in your church.

Step Five: *Read the Links in this Study Guide*—We have provided supplemental study links in the follow up section at the end of each lesson. These are mostly free resources that delve deeper into certain aspects of each lesson's subject.

Every ministry leader has a reading list. Add these articles to your list. That way, throughout the year, as you read some of these resources, you will reflect on the subject of abuse again. Part of staying sharp in any ministry area is repetition. By adding these links to your reading list, you will be making sure this video isn't the last time you think about abuse until you are mid-crisis.

Step Six: *Send Links to Specific Leaders*—As a ministry leader, your calling is to "equip the saints for the work of ministry" (Eph. 4:12). So, as you review the supplemental resources for each lesson, a primary question you should be asking is, "*Who* at our church needs to read this?"

Use this as an opportunity to encourage those leaders. Thank them for their faithful service. Pray for them and then tell them you prayed for them. This way an email with an article or video come across less as a "to-do list" from their ministry supervisor and more as a church leader investing in their contribution to God's kingdom through your church. Also, as a means of helping them own the material even more, ask them the very same question I'm asking you: "Who else do you think needs to read this?" Chances are, someone in their small group or ministry area also needs to read these resources.

To know which lessons are most pertinent to certain leaders in your church, head to Appendix B, where the lessons are indexed according to ministry area. The churchcares.com website makes it easy and efficient to email these leaders the video lessons they need for training.

Step Seven: *Post Resources on Abuse through the Church's Social Media Accounts*—We want this curriculum to do more than equip you, as a ministry leader. We want this resource to cultivate awareness that God loves the oppressed and wants to protect them through the church-at-large.

Here's the reality: what a pastor talks about in the pulpit or through social media is what congregation members think it's okay to struggle with at that church. If abuse is never mentioned, then "I must be the only one" is the belief of abuse victims in your church.

Here is one simple way to rectify that dilemma: schedule to post abuse resources in your church's social media accounts at a set interval. Reading an article or watching a video in the privacy of their home or phone feels safe. It becomes a way to realize that God cares, their church cares, and they don't have to continue to navigate this difficult journey alone.

HEAR FROM THE EXPERTS

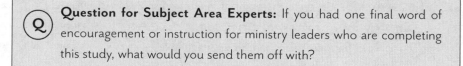

Question for Subject Area Experts: If you had one final word of encouragement or instruction for ministry leaders who are completing this study, what would you send them off with?

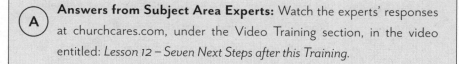

Answers from Subject Area Experts: Watch the experts' responses at churchcares.com, under the Video Training section, in the video entitled: *Lesson 12 – Seven Next Steps after this Training.*

Chris Moles: Congratulations on completing the curriculum. Your commitment to seeing this through encourages me so much. I believe pastors and church leaders must play a larger role in caring for victims and holding perpetrators accountable. There are no perfect interventions, you will make mistakes. My prayer is that we will be quick to own our missteps and mistakes, that we will repent of ways in which we have harmed others or revictimized those we are called to serve, and that we will be humble enough to course correct when needed, and ask for help from the larger body of Christ. Lastly, I want to encourage you to continue learning. Read good books on abuse prevention and intervention, ask questions of experts and service providers, attend trainings and seminars, and above all cover this matter and you church's response in prayer. "May the God of all hope fill you with joy and peace."

Darby Strickland: We have the opportunity to be representative of God. Our words, actions, and responses are ways that victims will learn about God and His heart for them. We need to be humble and gentle helpers seeking to embody Jesus. Jesus comes near to the suffering and He is tender with them.

We should be mindful of the fact that Jesus, came into this world sacrificially, not holding His power and position over us, but instead, He is devoted and sacrificing. He is the anti-oppressor; He does not seek to rule over us, demand our affections, or subject us to His majesty. Instead Jesus woos us with His gentle and forgiving love. So much so that, Jesus was willing to be wounded, even to the point of death to display His love for us.

Embody these realities for victims, their oppressors have done the opposite—and harmed their them in unimaginable ways. Victims need to see Jesus' love on display. Hebrews 13:3 says "Remember them that are in bonds, as bound with them; them that are ill-treated, as being yourselves also in the body" (KJV). You are called to a redemptive role, that begins with your long-suffering alongside them. If we do this well, their story will become more than just about the abuse, it will be about Jesus and His redemption.

At times loving this way will be costly to us personally, just as it cost Jesus, but it is beautiful because it embodies God's heart for His children. Doing ministry in this way will not only transform victims, but also you and your church.

Diane Langberg: To those of you who have been victimized—some of you by both your abuser and by the church's response: whenever God's people fail to speak truth, expose the deeds of darkness to light, and function as a refuge for the afflicted and needy—they have not only failed you but have failed our God as well, for they look nothing like Him.

Pastors, leaders, elders—when you fail victims, you are also failing the abusers. Those who perpetrate abuse and violence among the people of our God are mightily deceived and in bondage to their deceptions. When we fail to turn on the light and expose what it is hidden from others and themselves, it is a failure of love. It is the equivalent of knowing a loved one has cancer and helping them deny its presence. That cancer will inevitably spread and result in death. Yes, the treatment will be horrifyingly hard and long and result in losses. However, to agree to pretend with them that they are fine is a sentence of death.

Is the church of our Lord Jesus Christ willing to shed light in dark places and be a refuge for the brokenhearted and crushed? If she is not, then she is serving another God rather than the Holy One who became a babe. The voices of victims in our churches are in fact the voice of our God calling us to repentance and to faithfulness to *His ways*—not to our earthly kingdoms. I pray we will listen and follow no matter the cost.

Rachael Denhollander: I'm a survivor who has been through sexual abuse inside and outside of the church. I've been on the receiving end of very poor church responses, and the receiving end of very good ones. I've walked alongside many who can say the same.

I cannot stress enough how much damage church leaders can do to a survivor, and to their understanding of the gospel and Jesus Christ, if they do not know how to respond well to abuse and care for survivors. In each instance of my abuses and coming forward about them, the most painful aspects were how my churches responded. The greatest hindrance to my healing, was how churches speak about, and handled, abuse. I am far from alone in my experiences. Unfortunately, most survivors would echo what I have said.

But it is also true that my greatest refuge and healing came from properly understanding how Jesus sees abuse, and the incredible hope of the gospel. It is also true that some of my greatest comforts came from my churches that responded well.

Leaders, you can do incredible damage, and you need to feel that weight. But you also can do incredible good, and you should feel that hope.

Statistically, around a fourth of your congregation and your community have experienced sexual or domestic abuse. That's a huge number of people who desperately need hope. Everything an assault survivor needs is found in the redemptive work of Christ and the promise of that day when every tear is wiped away, and Christ returns to mete out justice. My prayer for you is that you will continue to grow in your heart to love as Christ did, and grow in your ability to bring the love and hope and justice of Christ, to those who are suffering. Redemption is a beautiful thing, and we are privileged to labor together for it.

Leslie Vernick: Church leaders must face something they find troublesome and that is the reality that some marriages cannot be saved. Not because God can't heal, but because people won't repent or do the hard work to change. Therefore marital trust cannot be repaired enough to live together safely, and that safety is not just physical safety. It's also emotional, mental, sexual and even spiritual safety.

Genuine reconciliation of a marriage that's been destructive and abusive takes more than saying "I'm sorry" or "I promise I won't do it again," especially when the sinful behavior has repeated itself over and over again in their relationship. It takes hard work over time to demonstrate the fruit of genuine repentance in real change. Sadly, the abuser is often unwilling to take responsibility or be accountable for long term change to take root.

Proverbs 18:5 reminds us, "It is not right to acquit the guilty or to deny justice to the innocent" (NLT). Sin has very real consequences. God wants His people to be merciful and forgive, but extending grace does not automatically remove negative consequences nor does it repair broken trust. To require a victim to live in an intimate relationship with an individual who has repeatedly caused him or her harm and is unchanged is not in keeping with the heart or counsel of God.

God does not care more about the sanctity of marriage than He does for the safety and sanity of the individuals within that relationship.

Samantha Kilpatrick: There is danger in viewing everything through the lens of liability exposure. In law practice, as a Christ follower, while I often have legal discussions surrounding liability, I always try to point the church to making the safety and care of victims a priority—not because of liability or mitigation, but because it is the right thing to do.

As a pastor and church leader, I urge you to be proactive in creating, reviewing, and enforcing policies, educate your staff and volunteers to be vigilant and to follow policies, get out in your community and find resources that will help you on this journey, and when you do receive a report of abuse, utilize those community contacts.

There are other proactive things that you can do to prepare yourself for these moments—educate yourself on abuse and trauma with secular and faith-based materials. Read and listen to stories of abuse—as hard as it is, you must expose yourself to the raw details of these stories in order to experience true sadness and grief for the person in front of you. Validate the courage and bravery of those who come forward and let them know you believe them. Avoid the common mistakes of interrogating and asking questions that are judgmental of an individual's behavior. Above all—protect the stories. The very fact that they are sharing is a step towards regaining some control and finding their voice.

Andrea Munford: Building relationships with law enforcement and community resources is crucial to providing necessary care and support to victims of abuse. It's important to know what you don't know and to have the help of professionals who can determine when a crime has been committed, and when additional resources are needed to ensure the safety of the victim, the church, and the community.

The difference between something illegal versus something immoral can be so obvious at times, but sometimes it's not so easily recognizable, and it's important to know that there are trained professionals that are not only available to help, but that they are invested in their community, which your church is part of. Seek out community police officers that work specifically in your area. Find out if there is a list of Christian service providers in your area, such as counselors, attorneys, and shelters. If not, consider joining with other churches and businesses to produce one.

And remember, being engaged in with professionals in the community shows them the importance of support by ministry leaders, it gives them witness to God working in the lives of the people they have to sworn to serve and protect, and it teaches them that God is working in their life as well, where they may not otherwise see this.

Mika Edmondson: The final word I would offer the church about addressing abuse is hope. As Zechariah prophesied about the salvation the Messiah would bring, he referred to God's people as "prisoners of hope." He said this during days of oppression, darkness, and pain when many of them were still in exile. We may often feel like that when it comes to abuse. The statistics on abuse in the church are heartbreaking. The church has often perpetuated worldly attitudes towards victims of abuse and in some cases even protected abusers. For victims and advocates, justice and deliverance can often seem elusive. Nevertheless, God's people are called prisoners of hope because the redemption that Christ obtained for us makes a claim upon us that no abuse or pattern of abuse can eradicate.

At the cross, Jesus Christ endured severe abuse at the hands of the church and the state, and when He was raised from the dead He revealed God's triumph over all sin, including the sin of abuse. As He ascended to the right hand of the Father, He raised His outstretched hands in blessing over His people to ensure our victory of the assaults of the enemy. Then Christ took up a ministry of intercession for all His people including those who are victims of abuse. And when He poured out His spirit, Christ gave us the power of His victory over abuse. This means that as we fight against sin, Christ is with us healing us from the guilt and shame of abuse. He is with us cleansing hearts and giving us a refuge from ongoing abuse. He is with us directing us and establishing justice for victims of abuse now until that justice is fully realized upon His return. We are prisoners of hope, not because we are a group of individuals able to pull ourselves out of the clutches of abuse. But because in the resurrected Christ we have a guarantee of our victory over every form of abuse, no matter how severe.

Karla Siu: As pastors and ministry leaders, you will undoubtedly enter into dark and difficult places when ministering to victims of abuse. Enter into these places with the power of God that brings salvation. Allow God's power, through His Holy Spirit, to work through your weakness and bear fruit.

Keep your eyes on Jesus, and focus on the transformative power of the gospel. As Isaiah 30:15 says, "In returning and rest you shall be saved; in quietness and in trust shall be your strength" (ESV).

When we acknowledge that God is already at work in this situation, and He's inviting us to come alongside the work He is already doing, we will not only *not lose hope* but we too will be transformed and encounter anew the *living God*.

KEY POINTS OF THIS LESSON

- Thank you for caring enough to complete this study and face the uncomfortable subject of abuse.
- Make sure key lay leaders in your church review the lessons relevant to their area of ministry.
- Look for ways to create awareness of quality abuse resources for those in your congregation.

FOLLOW UP RESOURCES

- Article: "Recommendations for Churches Dealing with Abuse" by Diane Langberg; http://www.dianelangberg.com/2019/02/recommendations-for-churches-dealing-with-abuse/

- Article: "When Prevention Fails: A Sexual Abuse Response Policy for Churches" by Brad Hambrick; http://bradhambrick.com/beyondprevention/

- Article: "Registered Sex Offender: A Sample Church Membership and Attendance Policy" by Brad Hambrick; http://bradhambrick.com/rso/

Appendix A

The purpose of this Appendix is to provide you with information regarding state laws on mandatory reporting of child abuse, statute of limitations for criminal acts of abuse, and age of consent laws. **The content in this appendix is provided for informational purposes only and is not legal advice.** It is important to remember that the laws in these areas are consistently updated or changed over time, so please consult with competent legal counsel regarding the application of these laws to any specific situation. All information provided in this Appendix was thoroughly researched and is current as of April 2019. At the time of publication, many states had legislation pending that, if passed, could change the information provided in this appendix.

Mandatory Reporting of Child Abuse

All states have mandatory reporting laws and systems to screen and investigate reports of abuse and neglect. The scope of this appendix is to provide you with an overview of each state's reporting law in regard to who must report, the legal standard required for reporting, what must be reported, and the penalty for failure to report. In addition, this appendix provides direct links to reporting in each individual state. In reviewing state laws on reporting, you will find that in some states, everyone is a mandated reporter and in others, there is a list of mandated reporters. No matter what your state's position, in all states you are *always permitted* to report even if you are not a mandated reporter. Finally, many states include clergy members in their list of mandated reporters. In this resource we have noted where the clergy-penitent privilege applies in regard to mandated reporting. Please be mindful that the clergy-penitent privilege is usually interpreted by courts to be very narrow in regard to reporting laws.

Statute of Limitations—Criminal

The statute of limitations refers to the maximum amount of time in which a victim and/or prosecutor may initiate criminal charges against an individual. In light of the fact that many crimes of sexual assault and abuse are not reported immediately, many states have recently started reviewing and seeking to amend their statute of limitations for these types of offenses. Currently there are a number of states that have pending legislation regarding this issue. Some states have decided to eliminate a statute of limitations for felonies altogether, while others have chosen to extend or allow other exceptions. Many states have adopted a DNA exception to their statute of limitations. This exception either extends or eliminates the statute of limitations for certain sexual offenses when there is DNA collected, preserved, and analyzed to confirm the identity of the offender. Oftentimes, if DNA is collected and an offender is not identified, it will toll the statute of limitations on that crime.

Age of Consent and Statutory Rape

Most states do not have a statutory rape statute per se; however, they do set an age of consent within their sexual assault statutes. Statutory rape is different from rape in that it is not by force or violence, but rather solely based upon sexual activity and the age of the victim. Until the age of consent is reached, the state maintains that those younger individuals do not have the capacity to consent to sexual activity. Thus, the sexual activity is non-consensual from a legal perspective. Due to the widespread sexual activity among teens, many states have opted to include close-in-age exemptions or what some call "Romeo and Juliet laws" in order to avoid criminal prosecution of two teenagers that are "consenting" to sexual activity. In many states, the age of consent is raised or the close-in-age exemption does not apply if the offender is a person responsible for the minor or in authority over the minor.

ALABAMA

Child Abuse Reporting

Statutes and Regulations: Ala. Code §§ 26-14-1 to 26-14-13 (2019) // Ala. Admin. Code r.660-5-34 (2019)

Who Must Report: Alabama statutes provide a list of mandated reporters which includes *members of the clergy*, medical personnel, mental health providers, social workers, childcare providers, school employees, and law enforcement. Please refer to Ala. Code § 26-14-3 for the complete list of mandated reporters.

What Must Be Reported: Physical, sexual, mental abuse and neglect by someone responsible for the health and welfare of the child.

Legal Standard: Reasonable Suspicion

Penalty for Failure to Report: Misdemeanor

State Resource Link: http://dhr.alabama.gov/services/Child_Protective_Services/Abuse_Neglect_Reporting.aspx

Application to Clergy: Ala. §26-14-3(f) states that "clergy shall not be required to report information gained solely in a confidential communication privileged pursuant to Rule 505 of the Alabama Rules of Evidence which communication shall continue to be privileged as provided by law."

Statute of Limitations for Criminal Prosecution

Statutes: Ala. Code §§ 15-3-1; 15-3-2; 15-3-5 (2019)

Felonies: For most felonies, prosecution must be commenced within five years of the commission of the crime. However, Ala. Code § 15-3-5 sets out some exemptions to this general rule. Specifically, there is no statute of limitations for any felony sex offense involving the use, threat of use, or attempted use of force; any felony sex offense involving serious physical injury, or any felony sex offense involving a victim under the age of sixteen.

Misdemeanors: For most misdemeanors, the statute of limitations is one year.

DNA Exception: No

Statutory Rape / Age of Consent

Statutes: Ala. Code §§ 13A-6-62 through and §13A-70 (2019)

In Alabama, an individual under the age of 16 is incapable of consenting to sexual contact. It is illegal to engage in sexual activity with an individual under the age of 16.

Age: 16

ALASKA

Child Abuse Reporting

Statutes and Regulations: Alaska Stat. §§ 47.17.010 through 47.17.290 (2019)

Who Must Report: Alaska statutes provide a list of mandated reporters which includes medical personnel, mental health providers, social workers, childcare providers, school employees, and law enforcement. Please refer to Alaska Stat. § 47.17.020 for the complete list of mandated reporters.

What Must Be Reported: Physical or mental injury, sexual abuse, sexual exploitation, neglect, or maltreatment of a child.

Legal Standard: Reasonable Cause to Suspect – by statute "means cause, based on all the facts and circumstances known to the person, that would lead a reasonable person to believe that something might be the case." Alaska Stat. § 47.17.290

Penalty for Failure to Report: Misdemeanor

State Resource Link: http://dhss.alaska.gov/ocs/Pages/childrensjustice/mandatoryreporting.aspx

Clergy/Parishioner Privilege: Statutes do not address.

Statute of Limitations for Criminal Prosecution

Statutes: Alaska Stat. § 12.10.010 (2019)

Felonies: For most felonies, prosecution must be commenced within 5 years of the commission of a felony; however, Alaska Stat. §12.10.010 enumerates felonies that do not have a statute of limitations and can be commenced at any time. They are as follows: felony sexual abuse of a minor, sexual assaults that are unclassified, Class A or Class B felonies, distribution of child pornography, and sex trafficking. In addition, sexual assault of an individual who is mentally incapable, incapacitated, or unaware has a ten-year statute of limitations.

Misdemeanors: Prosecution must be commenced within 5 years of the commission of a misdemeanor.

DNA Exception: No

Statutory Rape / Age of Consent

Statutes: Alaska Stat. §§ 11.41.434 through 11.41.440 (2019)

In Alaska, an individual under the age of 16 is incapable of consenting to sexual contact. It is illegal to engage in sexual activity with an individual under the age of 16. Alaska has a close-in-age exemption of less than three years. The age of consent is raised if the offender is in a position of authority in respect to the victim.

Age: 16

ARIZONA

Child Abuse Reporting

Statutes and Regulations: Ariz. Rev. Stat. §13-3620 (2019)

Who Must Report: Arizona statutes provide a list of mandated reporters which includes *members of the clergy*, medical personnel, mental health providers, social workers, childcare providers, school employees, law enforcement, and any other person who has responsibility for the care of a minor. Please refer to Ariz. Rev. Stat. §13-3620 for the complete list of mandated reporters.

What Must Be Reported: Physical injury, abuse, child abuse, sexual abuse, or neglect

Legal Standard: Reasonable Belief

Penalty for Failure to Report: Could be a misdemeanor or felony—See Ariz. Rev. Stat. §13-3620

State Resource Link: https://dcs.az.gov/report-child-abuse

Clergy Privilege: Yes—According to Ariz. Rev. Stat. §13-3620, the clergy privilege only applies "to the communication or confession and not to personal observations the member of the clergy . . . may otherwise make of the minor."

Statute of Limitations for Criminal Prosecution

Statutes: Ariz. Rev. Stat. § 13-107 (2019)

Felonies: For most felonies, the statute of limitations is seven years. However, there is no statute of limitations for violent sexual assault, or sex crimes that are listed as Class 2 felonies.

Misdemeanors: There is a one-year statute of limitations for misdemeanors.

DNA Exception: Yes. Ariz. Rev. Stat. §13-107(E) provides a tolling of the statute of limitations for serious offenses when the identity of the offender is unknown or offense is unknown.

Statutory Rape / Age of Consent

Statutes: Ariz. Rev. Stat. §13-1404 – 1405 (2019)

These statutes provide guidance on a number of age-related scenarios related to sexual abuse and sexual conduct involving minors. Each offense is specific to the age of offender, victim, and the difference of age between the two. For some offenses, the offender's relationship to the victim is also an element of the crime.

Age: 18

ARKANSAS

Child Abuse Reporting

Statutes and Regulations: Ark. Code Ann. §§12-18-101 through 12-18-911 (2019)

Who Must Report: Arkansas statutes provide a list of mandated reporters which includes *members of the clergy*, medical personnel, mental health providers, social workers, childcare providers, school employees, and law enforcement. Please refer to Ark. Code Ann. §12-18-402 for the complete list of mandated reporters.

What Must Be Reported: Physical, mental abuse, or neglect or abandonment by a parent, guardian, or caretaker. Sexual abuse by anyone.

Legal Standard: Reasonable Cause to Suspect

Penalty for Failure to Report: Misdemeanor

State Resource Link: https://ar.mandatedreporter.org/UserAuth/Login!loginPage.action;jsessionid=3A5FD60156ADD10CA235365D4E41BEC7

Clergy Privilege: Yes. This privilege applies when information is acquired through communication required to be kept confidential pursuant to religious discipline of relevant denomination or faith.

Statute of Limitations for Criminal Prosecution

Statutes: Ark. Code § 5-1-109 (2019)

Felonies: In Arkansas, there is no statute of limitations for rape of minor, sexual indecency with a child, first degree sex offense, second degree sex offense when victim is a minor, incest with minor, exploitation of child.

In addition, other felonies that are committed against a minor, the victim has until his/her twenty-eighth birthday to report (commence criminal action) the following offenses: sexual assault in the third degree, sexual assault in the fourth degree, endangering the welfare of a minor in the first degree, permitting abuse of a minor, and computer child pornography.

Misdemeanors: Misdemeanors carry a one-year statute of limitation. However, an exception exists for failure to notify by mandated reporter, extending the statute of limitations to ten-years after the child victim reaches the age of eighteen.

DNA Exception: Yes

Statutory Rape / Age of Consent

Statute: Ark. Code §5-14-124 through 127(2019)

These statutes provide guidance on a number of age-related scenarios related to sexual abuse and sexual conduct involving minors. Each offense is specific to the age of offender, victim, and the difference of age between the two. For some offenses, the offender's relationship to the victim is also an element of the crime.

Age: 16

CALIFORNIA

Child Abuse Reporting

Statutes and Regulations: Cal. Penal Code §§ 11164 through 11172 (2019)

Who Must Report: California statutes provide a list of mandated reporters which includes *members of the clergy,* medical personnel, mental health providers, social workers, childcare providers, school employees, and law enforcement. Please refer to Cal. Penal Code § 11166 for the complete list of mandated reporters.

What Must Be Reported: Physical, sexual, mental abuse or neglect

Legal Standard: Reasonable suspicion means "that it is objectively reasonable for a person to entertain a suspicion, based upon facts that could cause a reasonable person in a like position, drawing, when appropriate, on his or her training and experience, to suspect child abuse or neglect. 'Reasonable suspicion' does not require certainty that child abuse or neglect has occurred nor does it require a specific medical indication of child abuse or neglect; any 'reasonable suspicion' is sufficient." Cal. Penal Code § 11166(a)(1).

Penalty for Failure to Report: Misdemeanor

State Resource Link: http://www.cdss.ca.gov/Reporting/Report-Abuse/Child-Protective-Services

Clergy Privilege: Yes. The requirement for mandated reporting does not apply to a member of the clergy who has obtained information during a "penitential communication." See Cal. Penal Code § 11166(d).

Statute of Limitations for Criminal Prosecution

Statutes: Cal. Penal Code §§ 799, 801.1, 801.2, and 803 (2019)

Felonies: California has no statute of limitations for rapes committed on or after January 1, 2017 or rapes for which the statute of limitations has not run by January 1, 2017. For all other rapes and serious sex offenses, the statute of limitations is 10 years. Some sex offense crimes against minors allow for the action be commenced up until the victim's fortieth birthday (applies to crimes committed on or after January 1, 2015).

Misdemeanors: The statute of limitations for misdemeanors ranges from one to three years depending on seriousness of offense and age of victim.

DNA Exception: Yes

Statutory Rape / Age of Consent

Statute: Cal. Penal Code § 261.5 (2019) prohibits "unlawful sexual intercourse" with a minor. The difference in age between the parties will determine whether it is a misdemeanor or felony. The statute also sets civil penalties for adults who engage in unlawful sexual intercourse with minors.

Age: 18

COLORADO

Child Abuse Reporting

Statutes and Regulations: Colo. Rev. Stat. §§ 19-3-301 through 309 (2019)

Who Must Report: Colorado statutes provide a list of mandated reporters which includes *members of the clergy*, medical personnel, mental health providers, social workers, childcare providers, school employees, coaches, and law enforcement. Please refer to Colo. Rev. Stat. §19-3-304 for the complete list of mandated reporters.

What Must Be Reported: Physical, sexual or mental abuse by a parent, guardian, or legal custodian

Legal Standard: Reasonable Cause to Suspect

Penalty for Failure to Report: Misdemeanor

State Resource Link: http://co4kids.org

Clergy Exception: Yes. The privilege only applies to those communications that fall within the clergy-penitent privilege, but would not apply to information that rises to the level of reasonable cause acquired through other means.

Statute of Limitations for Criminal Prosecution

Statute: Colo. Rev. Stat. § 16-5-401

Felonies: In Colorado, there is no statute of limitations for any sex offense against a child. Most felonies have a three year statute of limitations; however, some felony sexual assault has a statute of limitations of twenty years.

Misdemeanors: The statute of limitations for general misdemeanors is eighteen months; however, for misdemeanor offenses charges as sexual assaults the action must be commenced within five years of the commission of the crime.

DNA Exception: Yes.

Statutory Rape / Age of Consent

Statutes: Colo. Rev. Stat. § 18-3-402 through 405.3 (2019) - These statutes provide guidance on a number of age-related scenarios related to sexual abuse and sexual conduct involving minors. Each offense is specific to the age of offender, victim, and the difference of age between the two. For some offenses, the offender's relationship to the victim is also an element of the crime.

Age: 17

CONNECTICUT

Child Abuse Reporting

Statutes and Regulations: Conn. Gen. Stat. § 17a-101(2019) // Conn. Agencies Reg. §17a-101k-1 through 17a-101k-16 (2019)

Who Must Report: Connecticut statutes provide a list of mandated reporters which includes *members of the clergy*, medical personnel, mental health providers, social workers, childcare providers, school employees, and law enforcement. Please refer to Conn. Gen. Stat. § 17a-101 for the complete list of mandated reporters.

What Must Be Reported: Physical, sexual, mental, neglect inflicted by a "responsible person"—parent, guardian, person entrusted with care.

Legal Standard: Reasonable Cause to Suspect

Penalty for Failure to Report: Misdemeanor

State Resource Link: https://portal.ct.gov/DCF/1-DCF/Reporting-Child-Abuse-and-Neglect

Clergy/Parishioner Privilege: The statutes do not address.

Statute of Limitations for Criminal Prosecution

Statutes: Conn. Gen. Stat. § 54-193 and § 54-193a

Felonies: Connecticut does not have a statute of limitation for sex crimes that are Class A felonies—first degree sexual assault of minor under the age of sixteen, first degree aggravated sexual assault of victim under age 16, and aggravated sexual assault of a minor. In addition, commercial sexual abuse of child under fifteen, trafficking persons, and employing a minor in obscene performance do not have a statute of limitations. Other crimes involving the sexual assault of a minor have a statute of limitations of either five years from date victim notified police or the victim's 48th birthday whichever is earlier. Other felony sex crimes charges that do not fit the above descriptions will have a five-year statute of limitations.

Misdemeanors: One year

DNA Exception: Yes.

Statutory Rape / Age of Consent

Statutes: Conn. Gen. Stat. §§ 53a-71 through 53a-73a (2019). These statutes provide guidance on a number of age-related scenarios related to sexual abuse and sexual conduct involving minors. Each offense is specific to the age of offender, victim, and the difference of age between the two. For some offenses, the offender's relationship to the victim is also an element of the crime.

Age: 16

DELAWARE

Child Abuse Reporting

Statutes: Del. Code Ann. tit. 16, §§ 901 through 914 (2019)

Who Must Report: Anyone who knows or in good faith suspects.

What Must Be Reported: Physical abuse, emotional abuse, torture, exploitation mistreatment, or maltreatment by person responsible for care custody or control of child. Sexual abuse by anyone.

Legal Standard: Good faith suspicion

Penalty for Failure to Report: Civil penalties up to $10,000, cost and attorney's fees.

State Resource Link: https://kids.delaware.gov/fs/fs_iseethesigns.shtml

Clergy Privilege: Yes, the privilege applies only to those communications that are part of the "sacramental confession."

Statute of Limitations for Criminal Prosecution

Statutes: Del. Code Ann. tit. 11 §205 (2019)

Felonies: In Delaware, there is no time limitation on Class A felonies (first degree rape). All other felonies have a five-year statute of limitations.

Misdemeanors: Varies from two to three years

DNA Exception: Yes

Statutory Rape / Age of Consent

Statutes: Del. Code Ann. tit. 11, §761, §768 through 772 (2019). These statutes provide guidance on a number of age-related scenarios related to sexual abuse and sexual conduct involving minors. Each offense is specific to the age of offender, victim, and the difference of age between the two. For some offenses, the offender's relationship to the victim is also an element of the crime.

Age: 16

"A child who has not yet reached that child's sixteenth birthday is deemed unable to consent to a sexual act with a person more than 4 years older than said child. Children who have not yet reached their twelfth birthday are deemed unable to consent to a sexual act under any circumstances." Del. Code Ann. tit. 11, §761.

DISTRICT OF COLUMBIA (D.C.)

Child Abuse Reporting

Statutes and Regulations: D.C. Code §§ 4-1321.01 through 4-1321.07

Who must report: District of Columbia statutes provide a list of mandated reporters which includes medical personnel, mental health providers, social workers, childcare providers, school employees, and law enforcement. Please refer to Alaska Stat. § D.C. Code § 4-1321.02 for the complete list of mandated reporters.

Note: At the time of this publication legislation is pending to include clergy in the list of mandated reporters.

What Must Be Reported: Physical, sexual, mental abuse and neglect.

Legal Standard: Reasonable Cause to Suspect

Penalty for Failure to Report: Misdemeanor

State Resource Link: https://cfsa.dc.gov/service/report-child-abuse-and-neglect

Clergy/Parishioner Privilege: Yes, if information from confession or penitential communication.

Statute of Limitations for Criminal Prosecution

Statutes: DC Code § 23-113 (2019)

Felonies: The statute of limitations for felony sex abuse varies from ten-years to fifteen years. Most other felonies have a six year statute of limitations. For some felony sex abuse crimes, the time does not start to run until the child victim reaches the age of twenty-one.

Note: At the time of this publication, legislation is pending to remove the statute of limitations from a number of felony sex abuse crimes.

Misdemeanors: Three years

Statutory Rape / Age of Consent

Statutes: DC Code 22-3008 through 22-3010.01 (2019). These statutes define child sexual abuse and sexual abuse of a minor. Child sexual abuse requires that the offender be at least four years older than the child (one not yet sixteen) and engage in sexual activity. Sexual abuse of a minor occurs when the offender is at least eighteen years old, in a significant relationship with a minor, and engages in sexual activity with that minor.

Age: 16

FLORIDA

Child Abuse Reporting

Statutes and Regulations: Fla. Stat. §§ 39.201 through 39.206 (2019)

Who Must Report: Everyone

What Must Be Reported: Physical, sexual, mental abuse, neglect by parent, guardian, caretaker, or other responsible adult. Any abuse by any adult other than parent, guardian or caretaker.

Legal Standard: Reasonable Cause to Suspect

Penalty for Failure to Report: Felony

State Resource Link: https://www.dcf.state.fl.us/service-programs/abuse-hotline/frequently-asked-questions.shtml

Clergy Privilege: Yes. Under Florida law, communication with clergy is considered "confidential if made privately for the purpose of seeking spiritual counsel . . ." Fla. Stat. §39.204 and Fla. Stat. §90.505

Statute of Limitations for Criminal Prosecution

Statutes: Fla. Stat. § 775.15

Felonies: There is no statute of limitations for the most serious felony sexual battery on a victim under the age of eighteen. Other felony sexual battery crimes have statute of limitations that may range from three to eight years

Misdemeanors: One to two years.

DNA Exception: Yes, for crimes committed after 2006.

Statutory Rape / Age of Consent

Statutes: Fla. Stat. §794.05 (2019). An individual who is twenty-four years old or older is prohibited from engaging in sexual activity with a sixteen or seventeen year old.

Fla. Stat. §800.04 (2019). This statute prohibits lewd and lascivious offenses committed on individuals less than sixteen years of age.

Age: Eighteen is the general consensus, but the language in case law and § 800.04 seem to indicate sixteen.

GEORGIA

Child Abuse Reporting

Statute: Ga. Code Ann. §19-7-5 (2019)

Who Must Report: Georgia statutes provide a list of mandated reporters which includes medical personnel, counselors, social workers, school employees, and law enforcement. Please refer to Ga. Code Ann. §19-7-5(c) for the full list of mandated reporters. While clergy is not specifically listed here, clergy is mentioned in subsection (g) of the statute, and one could argue that it implies a duty to report for clergy in certain circumstances outside the privilege.

What Must Be Reported: Physical, mental, sexual abuse, neglect by parent or caretaker.

Legal Standard: Reasonable Cause to Believe

Penalty for Failure to Report: Misdemeanor

State Resource Link: https://dfcs.georgia.gov/child-abuse-neglect

Clergy Privilege: Yes. A "member of the clergy shall not be required to report child abuse reported solely within the context of confession or other similar communication required to be kept confidential under church doctrine or practice. When a clergy member receives information about child abuse from any other source, the clergy member shall comply with the reporting requirements of this Code section, even though the clergy member may have also received a report of child abuse from the confession of the perpetrator." Ga. Code Ann. §19-7-5(g)

Statute of Limitations for Criminal Prosecution

Statutes: Ga. Code §§ 17-3-1 through 17-3-2.1

Felonies: There is no statute of limitations for rape, aggravated child molestation, aggravated sodomy, and aggravated sexual battery when DNA has established the identity of the offender. In addition, there is no statute of limitations for crimes committed after July 1, 2012, where the victim is less than 16 years of age and is the victim of trafficking for the purpose of sexual servitude, first degree cruelty to a child, rape, aggravated sodomy, child molestation enticement of child for indecent purposes, or incest. Forcible rape has a statute of limitations of 15 years. Most other felonies carry a 4 year statute of limitations.

Misdemeanors: Two years

DNA Exception: Yes, for specified offenses.

Statutory Rape / Age of Consent

Statute: Ga. Code §16-6-3 (2019) statutory rape is a felony, and it occurs when an individual engages in sexual intercourse with someone under the age of 16. If the victim is at least 14 years old but not yet 16 years old, and the offender is 18 years old or younger, and no more than four years older than the victim, then the crime is a misdemeanor.

Age: 16

HAWAII

Child Abuse Reporting

Statutes and Regulations: Haw. Rev. Stat. §§ 350-1 through 350-7 (2019)

Who Must Report: Hawaii statutes provide a list of mandated reporters which includes medical personnel, counselors, childcare providers, recreational/sports activities providers, social workers, school employees, and law enforcement. Please refer to Haw. Rev. Stat. § 350-1.1(a) for the full list of mandated reporters.

What Must Be Reported: Physical, sexual, mental abuse, or neglect, by person related to, residing with or responsible for the child.

If the child has been the victim of sexual contact.

Legal Standard: Reason to Believe

Penalty for Failure to Report: Misdemeanor

State Resource Link: http://humanservices.hawaii.gov/ssd/home/child-welfare-services/

Clergy Privilege: The statutes do not address.

Statute of Limitations for Criminal Prosecution

Statutes: Haw. Rev. Stat. § 701-108(1)

Felonies: The crimes of sexual assault in the first and second degrees and continuous sexual assault of a minor under the age of fourteen years do not have a statute of limitations and may be commenced at any time. Other felonies have a three to six year statute of limitations.

Misdemeanors: Two years

DNA Exception: Yes

Statutory Rape / Age of Consent

Statutes: Haw. Rev. Stat. §§ 707-730 through 707-733.6 (2019). These statutes provide guidance on a number of age-related scenarios related to sexual abuse and sexual conduct involving minors. Each offense is specific to the age of offender, victim, and the difference of age between the two. For some offenses, the offender's relationship to the victim is also an element of the crime.

Age: 16

IDAHO

Child Abuse Reporting

Statutes: Idaho Code Ann. §§ 16-1602 through 16-1607 (2019)

Who Must Report: Everyone

What Must Be Reported: Physical, sexual, mental, abandonment, or neglect.

Legal Standard: Reason to Believe

Penalty for Failure to Report: Misdemeanor

State Resource Link: https://healthandwelfare.idaho.gov/Children/AbuseNeglect/
ChildProtectionContactPhoneNumbers/tabid/475/Default.aspx

https://healthandwelfare.idaho.gov/Portals/0/Children/AbuseNeglect/CARTF
CareEnough.pdf

Clergy/Parishioner Privilege: Yes. The notification requirements do not apply to communications made within the ecclesiastical capacity and the church has to meet certain requirements of the statute.

Statute of Limitations for Criminal Prosecution

Statutes: Idaho Code §§ 19-401; 19-402

Felonies: The crimes of rape and sexual abuse of child may be commenced at any time and do not have a statute of limitations. Most other felonies have a five year statute of limitations.

Misdemeanors: One year

DNA Exception: No

Statutory Rape / Age of Consent

Statutes: Idaho Code § 18-6101 (2019) prohibits sexual intercourse with individuals under the age of 16 years of age by an individual who is 18 years old or older; it also prohibits sexual intercourse with a 16 or 17 year old if the perpetrator is three years or more older than the victim.

Age: 18

ILLINOIS

Child Abuse Reporting

Statutes and Regulations: 325 Ill. Comp. Stat. Ann. 5/1 through 5/11.8 (2019) // 89 Ill. Adm. Code 300.30 – 300.40 (2019)

Who Must Report: Illinois statutes provide a list of mandated reporters which includes *members of the clergy,* medical personnel, counselors, childcare providers, recreational/ sports activities providers, social workers, school employees, and law enforcement. Please refer to 325 Ill. Comp. Stat. Ann. 5/4 for the full list of mandated reporters.

What Must Be Reported: Physical, sexual, mental abuse, or neglect inflicted by parent or family member, caretaker, parent's paramour, other person responsible for child's welfare (educator, coach, health provider) or someone residing with the child.

Legal Standard: Reasonable Cause to Believe

Penalty for Failure to Report: Misdemeanor

State Resource Link: https://www2.illinois.gov/dcfs/Pages/default.aspx

Clergy Privilege: Yes. Members of the clergy "shall not be compelled to disclose a confession or admission made to him or her in his or her professional character or as a spiritual advisor." See 89 Ill. Adm. Code 300.30((b)(5)(c) and 735 Ill. Comp. Stat. Ann. 5/8-803.

Statute of Limitations for Criminal Prosecution

Statutes: 720 Ill. Comp. Stat. Ann. 5/3-5 (2019) // 720 Ill. Comp. Stat. Ann. 5/3-6 (2019)

Felonies: Crimes involving sexual conduct or penetration (where the perpetrators DNA profile was obtained and entered into the system within ten-years; see other reporting requirements in the statute) may be commenced at any time and do not have a statute of limitations. In addition, felony sexual assault and abuse crimes of victims under age 18 may be commenced at any time and do not have a statute of limitations. For the crimes of involuntary servitude, involuntary servitude of minor for sexual purposes, and trafficking in persons, the action may be brought within 25 years of the victim reaching the age of 18. For other felony crimes not designated in the statutes, the statute of limitations is three years.

Misdemeanors: One year and six months; except misdemeanor sexual abuse where victim is younger than 18, action may commence within 10 years of the victim's eighteenth birthday.

DNA Exception: Yes

Statutory Rape / Age of Consent

Statutes: 720 Ill. Comp. Stat. Ann. 5/11-1.50 (2019) – this statute prohibits criminal sexual abuse which occurs when an individual under the age of 17 engages in sexual activity with a victim between the ages of 9 and 16 years of age or where the victim is between 13 and 16 and the offender is within five years of the victim's age.

720 Ill. Comp. Stat. Ann. 5/11-1.50 (2019) – the statute prohibits aggravated criminal sexual abuse. This statute provides guidance on a number of age-related scenarios related to sexual abuse and sexual conduct involving minors with specific details regarding the age of offender, victim, and the difference of age between the two. For some offenses, the offender's relationship to the victim is also an element of the crime.

Age: 17

INDIANA

Child Abuse Reporting

Statutes and Regulations: Ind. Code Ann. §§ 31-33-5-1 through 31-33-5-5 (2019)

Who Must Report: Everyone

What Must Be Reported: Physical, sexual, mental abuse or neglect.

Legal Standard: Reason to Believe

Penalty for Failure to Report: Misdemeanor

State Resource Link: https://www.in.gov/dcs/2971.htm

Clergy Privilege: The privilege may exist but it is not clear. Ind. Code Ann. § 31-32-11-1 specifically names a number of privileged relationships that are not grounds for excluding evidence in child abuse cases. Clergy-penitent is not one of them, so one may be able to assume it is intact. Please seek legal counsel in your state for the answer to this question.

Statute of Limitations for Criminal Prosecution

Statutes: Ind. Code § 35-41-4-2 (2019)

Felonies: A charge of aggravated rape may be commenced at any time and does not have a statute of limitations. Most other felonies have a 5 year statute of limitations. For the crimes of child molestation, child solicitation, child seduction, and incest charges must be filed before the victim's thirty-first birthday.

Misdemeanors: 2 years

DNA Exception: Yes

Statutory Rape / Age of Consent

Statutes: Ind. Code § 35-42-4-9 (2019) - This statute provides guidance on a number of age-related scenarios related to sexual abuse and sexual conduct involving minors with specific details regarding the age of offender, victim, and the difference of age between the two. For some offenses, the offender's relationship to the victim is also an element of the crime.

Age: 16

IOWA

Child Abuse Reporting

Statutes: Iowa Code §§ 232.67 through 232.75 (2019)

Who Must Report: Iowa statutes provide a list of mandated reporters which includes medical personnel, counselors, childcare providers, social workers, school employees, and law enforcement. Please refer to Iowa Code §§ 232.69 for the full list of mandated reporters.

What Must Be Reported: Physical, sexual, mental abuse or neglect by a person responsible for care of the child.

Commission of a sexual offense by person responsible for the care or the child or person who is fourteen years old or older who resides in the home with the child.

Legal Standard: Reasonable Belief

Penalty for Failure to Report: Misdemeanor

State Resource Link: https://dhs.iowa.gov/child-abuse

Clergy Privilege: Statutes do not address.

Statute of Limitations for Criminal Prosecution

Statutes: Iowa Code §§ 802.2 through 802.4 (2019)

Felonies: Child sex abuse crimes must commence within ten years of child's eighteenth birthday. Other felony crimes have a statute of limitations of three years.

Misdemeanors: One to three years depending on seriousness.

DNA Exception: Yes

Statutory Rape / Age of Consent

Statutes: Iowa Code §§ 709.2 through 709.15 (2019) These statutes provide guidance on a number of age-related scenarios related to sexual abuse and sexual conduct involving minors with specific details regarding the age of offender, victim, and the difference of age between the two. For some offenses, the offender's relationship to the victim is also an element of the crime.

Age: 16

KANSAS

Child Abuse Reporting

Statutes and Regulations: Kan. Stat. Ann. § 38-2223 (2019)

Who Must Report: Kansas statutes provide a list of mandated reporters which includes medical personnel, counselors, childcare providers, emergency medical personnel, social workers, school employees, and law enforcement. Please refer to Kan. Stat. Ann. § 38-2223 for the full list of mandated reporters.

What Must Be Reported: Physical, mental, emotional abuse, neglect, or sexual abuse.

Legal Standard: Reason to Suspect

Penalty for Failure to Report: Misdemeanor

State Resource Link: http://www.dcf.ks.gov/pages/report-abuse-or-neglect.aspx

Clergy Privilege: The statutes do not address.

Statute of Limitations for Criminal Prosecution

Statutes: Kan. Stat. § 21-5107 (2019)

Felonies: A charge of rape may be commenced at any time and it does not have statute of limitations. For other violent felony sex crimes, the statute of limitations is ten years from the date of commission of the crime or if the victim is under the age of 18, then the charge must be brought within ten years of the eighteenth birthday. The statute for other felonies is five years.

Misdemeanors: One to three years, depending on seriousness.

DNA Exception: Yes

Statutory Rape / Age of Consent

Statutes: Kan. Stat. § 21-5503 (2019) – This statute makes it illegal to engage in sexual intercourse with a child under the age of fourteen.

Kan. Stat. § 21-5506 (2019) – This statute covers a range of illegal sexual activity with children under the age of 16. Sexual intercourse with a child who is 14 years of age but less than 16 years of age is illegal.

Kan. Stat. § 21-5507 (2019) – This statute prohibits "voluntary" sexual acts with children between the ages of 14 and 16 years of age.

Age: 16

KENTUCKY

Child Abuse Reporting

Statute: Ky. Rev. Stat. §§ 620.030 (2019)

Who Must Report: Everyone

What Must Be Reported: Physical, sexual, mental abuse, neglect, or human trafficking.

Legal Standard: Reasonable Cause to Believe

Penalty for Failure to Report: Misdemeanor

State Resource Link: https://chfs.ky.gov/agencies/dcbs/dpp/cpb/Pages/default.aspx and https://prdweb.chfs.ky.gov/ReportAbuse/home.aspx

Clergy Privilege: Yes. See Ky. Rev. Stat. § 620.030(4).

Statute of Limitations for Criminal Prosecution

Statutes: Ky. Rev. Stat. § 500.050 (2019)

Felonies: No statute of limitations on any felony sex crime.

Misdemeanors: One year

Statutory Rape / Age of Consent

Statutes: Ky. Rev. Stat. § 510.020 (2019)—This statute sets the standard for consent as it relates to age. An individual under the age of 16, is incapable of consent. In addition, a 16 or 17 year old is not capable of consenting when the actor is at least ten years older.

Ky. Rev. Stat. § 510.040 through 510.140 (2019)—These statutes provide guidance on a number of age-related scenarios related to sexual assault, abuse and sexual conduct involving minors with specific details regarding the age of offender, victim, and the difference of age between the two. For some offenses, the offender's relationship to the victim is also an element of the crime.

Age: 16

LOUISIANA

Child Abuse Reporting

Statutes: La. Child. Code Ann. art. 603 through 611 (2019) // La. Rev. Stat. Ann. § 14:403 (2019)

Who Must Report: Louisiana statutes provide a list of mandated reporters which includes *members of the clergy*, medical personnel, mental health providers, social workers, childcare providers, school employees, coaches, and law enforcement. Please refer to La. Child. Code Ann. art. 603(17) for the full list of mandated reporters.

What Must Be Reported: Physical abuse, sexual abuse, mental abuse, or neglect.

Legal Standard: Reasonable Cause to Believe

Penalty for Failure to Report: Misdemeanor

State Resource Link: http://www.dcfs.louisiana.gov/index.cfm?md=pagebuilder&tmp%E2%80%8B=home&nid=380&pid=109#undefined

Clergy Privilege: Yes. See La. Rev. Stat. Ann. § 14:403(B). However, La. Child. Code Ann. art. 603(17)(c) urges members of the clergy "to encourage that person to report the allegations to the appropriate authorities."

Statute of Limitations for Criminal Prosecution

Statutes: La. Crim. Proc. Code Ann. art. 571 through (2019)

Felonies: A charge for first or second-degree rape may be commenced at any time and does not have a statute of limitations. There are a number of sex offenses that have a thirty-year statute of limitations, and if the victim was under the age of 17 when the crime was committed, the thirty-year period will begin to run on the eighteenth birthday. Other felonies in this state have varying statutes of limitations ranging from four to six years.

Misdemeanors: Two years

DNA Exception: Yes

Statutory Rape / Age of Consent

Statutes: La. Rev. Stat. Ann. § 14.80 (2019) - This statute prohibits felony carnal knowledge of a juvenile. The statute provides guidance age of the victim as related to age of the offender in regard to sexual conduct.

La. Rev. Stat. Ann. §§ 14:80.1 through 14-81.5 (2019) provides guidance on a number of other sex offenses affecting minors such as pornography, sexting, computer solicitation, and other indecent behaviors.

Age: 17

MAINE

Child Abuse Reporting

Statutes and Regulations: Me. Rev. Stat. tit. 22 §§ 4009 through 4011-A (2019)

Who Must Report: Maine statutes provide a list of mandated reporters which includes *members of the clergy*, medical personnel, mental health providers, social workers, child-care providers, school employees, camp counselors, coaches, and law enforcement. Please refer to Me. Rev. Stat. tit. 22 § 4011-A(1)(A) for the complete list of mandated reporters.

What Must Be Reported: Abuse, neglect, or suspicious death.

Legal Standard: Reasonable Cause to Suspect

Penalty for Failure to Report: Civil Penalties

State Resource Link: https://www.maine.gov/dhhs/ocfs/cw/reporting_abuse.shtml

Clergy Privilege: Members of the clergy are mandated reporters and must report "information as a result of clerical professional work except for information received during confidential communications." See Me. Rev. Stat. tit. 22 § 4011-A(1)(A)(27).

Statute of Limitations for Criminal Prosecution

Statutes: Me. Rev. Stat. tit. 17-A, § 8

Felonies: For crimes such as incest; unlawful sexual contact; sexual abuse of a minor; rape or gross sexual assault where the victim is less than 16 years of age, there is no statue of limitations. For other felony sex crimes, the statute of limitations varies between three and eight years depending on the seriousness of the offense.

Misdemeanors: Three years

DNA Exception: No

Statutory Rape / Age of Consent

Statutes: Me. Rev. Stat. tit. 17, §254, §255A, §258, §260. These statutes provide guidance on age-related scenarios related to sexual assault, abuse and sexual conduct involving minors with specific details regarding the age of offender, victim, and the difference of age between the two.

Age: 16

MARYLAND

Child Abuse Reporting

Statutes and Regulations: Md. Code Ann. Family Law § 5-704 through 5-708 (2019)

Who Must Report: Everyone

What Must Be Reported: Physical or mental abuse or neglect by a parent, family member, household member, person with responsibility for care or authority over the child.

Sexual abuse by anyone

Legal Standard: Reason to Believe

Penalty for Failure to Report: Not stated

State Resource Link: http://dhs.maryland.gov/child-protective-services/reporting-suspected-child-abuse-or-neglect/

Clergy Privilege: Yes. A member of the clergy does not have to report if "the communication was made to the minister, clergyman, or priest in a professional character in the course of discipline enjoined by the church to which the minister, clergyman, or priest belongs; and the minister, clergyman, or priest is bound to maintain the confidentiality of that communication under canon law, church doctrine, or practice." Md. Code Ann. Family Law § 5-705(a)(3).

Statute of Limitations for Criminal Prosecution

Case Law: Massey v. State, 320 Md. 605, 610, 579 A.2d 265, 267 (Md. 1990); *State v. Renfro,* 223 Md. App. 779 (2015), cert. denied, 445 Md. 6, 122 A.3d 976 (2015)

Felonies: Maryland has no statute of limitations on felonies.

Misdemeanors: One to three years

DNA Exception: No

Statutory Rape / Age of Consent

Statutes: Md. Crim. Law Code Ann. §§ 3-304 through 308 (2019). These statutes provide guidance on age-related scenarios related to sexual assault, abuse and sexual conduct involving minors with specific details regarding the age of offender, victim, and the difference of age between the two.

Age: 16

MASSACHUSETTS

Child Abuse Reporting

Statutes: Mass. Gen. Laws ch.119 § 21 (2019)   //   Mass. Gen. Laws ch.119 § 51A (2019)

Who Must Report: Massachusetts statutes provide a list of mandated reporters which includes *members of the clergy, church employees who work with children,* medical personnel, mental health providers, social workers, childcare providers, school employees, and law enforcement. Please refer to Mass. Gen. Laws ch.119 § 21 for the complete list of mandated reporters

What Must Be Reported: Physical abuse, sexual abuse, emotional abuse, or neglect.

Legal Standard: Reasonable Cause to Believe

Penalty for Failure to Report: Fine and/or imprisonment

State Resource Link: https://www.mass.gov/how-to/report-child-abuse-or-neglect

Clergy Privilege: Yes. Member of the clergy "need not report information solely gained in a confession or similarly confidential communication in other religious faiths." However, if the information is gained in some other capacity the member of the clergy must report. See Mass. Gen. Laws ch.119 § 51A(j).

Statute of Limitations for Criminal Prosecution

Statutes: Mass. Gen. Laws ch. 277 § 63 (2019)

Felonies: For serious felony sexual offenses involving children, charge may be filed at any time, but if more than twenty-seven years later there are some requirements in order to bring charges. A charge for rape may be filed within fifteen years of the commission of the crime. If the victim is under the age of 16, the statute of limitations does not begin to run until the sixteenth birthday. Other felonies have a six year statute of limitations.

Misdemeanors: Six years

DNA Exception: No

Statutory Rape / Age of Consent

Statute: Mass. Gen. Laws ch. 265 § 23A (2019.) Massachusetts prohibits sexual intercourse with a child under the age of 16, if there is more than a five year age difference and the victim is under the age of 12 or if there is more than a ten-year age difference and the victim is between the age of 12 and 16 years of age.

See also Mass. Gen. Laws ch. 272 § 4 regarding enticing a person "of chaste life" under the age of eighteen.

Note: At the time of publication, legislation is pending that may change the age differences and penalties of the above referenced statutes.

Age: 16

MICHIGAN

Child Abuse Reporting

Statutes and Regulations: Mich. Comp. Laws §§ 722.621 through 722.633 (2019)

Who Must Report: Michigan statutes provide a list of mandated reporters which includes *members of the clergy*, medical personnel, mental health providers, social workers, childcare providers, school employees, and law enforcement. Please refer to Mich. Comp. Laws § 722.623 for the complete list of mandated reporters.

What Must Be Reported: Physical abuse, mental abuse, sexual abuse by parent, teacher, guardian member of the clergy, or person responsible for child's health or welfare.

Legal Standard: Reasonable Cause to Suspect

Penalty for Failure to Report: Civil liability and misdemeanor

State Resource Link: https://www.michigan.gov/mdhhs/0,5885,7-339-73971_7119_50648_7193---,00.html

Clergy Privilege: Yes. Members of the clergy are not required to report information received "in a confession or similarly confidential communication." However, the member of the clergy remains a mandatory reporter for any information received in any other capacity. See Mich. Comp. Laws § 722.631.

Statute of Limitations for Criminal Prosecution

Statutes: Mich. Comp. Laws § 767.24 (2019)

Felonies: In Michigan there is no statute of limitations for first degree criminal sexual conduct. For some felony sexual offenses involving minors, the statute of limitation ranges from ten to fifteen years of by the twenty-first or twenty-eighth birthday whichever is later. For other felonies the statute of limitations is six years.

Misdemeanors: Six years

DNA Exception: Yes

Statutory Rape / Age of Consent

Statutes: Mich. Comp. Laws §§ 750.520b through 520e (2019). These statutes address criminal sexual conduct with individuals under the age of 16. Michigan law prohibits sexual penetration and conduct with individuals under the age of 16. The degree and severity of the offense depends on the age difference, the acts committed, and the relationship between the offender and the victim.

Age: 16

MINNESOTA

Abuse Reporting

Statutes: Minn. Stat. § 626.556 through 626.556.1 (2019)

Who Must Report: Minnesota statutes provide a list of mandated reporters which includes *members of the clergy*, medical personnel, mental health providers, social workers, childcare providers, school employees, and law enforcement. Please refer to Minn. Stat. § 626.556 (Subd. 3) for the complete list of mandated reporters.

What Must Be Reported: Physical abuse, mental abuse, sexual abuse, or neglect by any person responsible for the child's care.

Legal Standard: Reason to Believe

Penalty for Failure to Report: Misdemeanor

State Resource Link: https://mn.gov/dhs/report-abuse/

https://www.dowr.org/img/Reporting%20Child%20Abuse%20and%20Neglect%20 1_16.pdf

Clergy/Parishioner Privilege: Yes. Members of the clergy are not required to report "information [acquired] while engaged in ministerial duties." See Minn. Stat. § 626.556(Subd. 3)(a)(2).

Statute of Limitations for Criminal Prosecution

Statutes: Minn. Stat. § 628.26 (2019)

Felonies: For crimes of trafficking of individuals under the age of 18, the charge may commence at any time and there is not a statute of limitations. For sexual offenses where the victim is under the age of 18, the statute of limitations is nine years or three years after reported to law enforcement, whichever occurs later. For other felonies, the statute of limitations varies between three and six years.

Note: At the time of publication, legislation is pending to eliminate the statute of limitations for some sexual offense crimes.

Misdemeanors: Three years

DNA Exception: Yes

Statutory Rape / Age of Consent

Statutes: Minn. Stat. §§ 609.341 through 609.3451 (2019). These statutes prohibit sexual intercourse or contact with individuals under the age of 16. The statutes define the degrees of the crime based on age of victim, age of offender, the difference in age, and relationship between the two.

Age: 16

MISSISSIPPI

Child Abuse Reporting

Statutes: Miss. Code. Ann. §§ 43-21-353 through 43-21-357 (2019)

Who Must Report: Everyone

What Must Be Reported: Physical, sexual, mental abuse, or neglect

Legal Standard: Reasonable Cause to Suspect

Penalty for Failure to Report: Fine and/or imprisonment

State Resource Link: https://www.mdcps.ms.gov/report-child-abuse-neglect/

Clergy Privilege: The statutes do not address.

Statute of Limitations for Criminal Prosecution

Statutes: Miss. Code § 99-1-5

Felonies: The crimes of rape and felony sexual abuse may be brought at any time, and they do not have a statute of limitations. The statute of limitations for other felonies is two years.

Misdemeanors: Two years

DNA Exception: No

Statutory Rape / Age of Consent

Statutes: Miss. Code Ann. § 97-3-65 and § 97-3-95 (2019). These statutes prohibit sexual intercourse or contact with individuals under the age of 16. The statutes define the degrees of the crime based on age of victim, age of offender, the difference in age, and relationship between the two.

Age: 16

MISSOURI

Child Abuse Reporting

Statutes and Regulations: Mo. Rev. Stat. §§ 210-110 through 210-140 (2019) // Mo. Rev. Stat. § 352.400 (2019)

Who Must Report: Missouri statutes provide a list of mandated reporters which includes *members of the clergy*, medical personnel, mental health providers, social workers, childcare providers, school employees, law enforcement, or any *"other person with responsibility for the care of children."* Please refer to Mo. Rev. Stat. §§ 210.115 (1) for the complete list of mandated reporters.

What Must Be Reported: Physical, emotional, sexual abuse, or neglect by person responsible for the care, custody, and control of the child.

Sex trafficking of a child.

Legal Standard: Reasonable Cause to Suspect

Penalty for Failure to Report: Misdemeanor

State Resource Link: https://dss.mo.gov/cd/keeping-kids-safe/can.htm

Clergy/Parishioner Privilege: Yes. Members of the clergy "shall not be required to report concerning a privileged communication made . . . in [their] professional capacity. See Mo. Rev. Stat. § 352.400 and § 210.140.

Statute of Limitations for Criminal Prosecution

Statutes: Mo. Rev. Stat. §§ 556.036 through 556.037 (2019)

Felonies: The crimes of rape, sodomy, and felony sex offenses against person 18 years of age or younger may be commenced at any time and do not have a statute of limitations. Most other felonies have a three-year statute of limitations.

Misdemeanors: One year

DNA Exception: Yes

Statutory Rape / Age of Consent

Statutes: Mo. Rev. Stat. §§ 566.032 through 566.034 (2019). These statutes prohibit sexual intercourse or contact with individuals under the age of 17. The statutes define the degrees of the crime based on age of victim, age of offender, the difference in age, and relationship between the two.

Age: 17

MONTANA

Child Abuse Reporting

Statutes and Regulations: Mont. Code Ann. § 41-3-102 (2019) // Mont. Code Ann. §§ 41-3-201 through 41-3-207 (2019)

Who Must Report: Montana statutes provide a list of mandated reporters which includes *members of the clergy*, medical personnel, mental health providers, social workers, school employees, and law enforcement. Please refer to Mont. Code Ann. § 41-3-201(2) for the complete list of mandated reporters.

What Must Be Reported: Physical abuse, sexual abuse, mental abuse, or neglect by anyone.

Legal Standard: Reasonable Cause to Suspect

Penalty for Failure to Report: Civil liability and Misdemeanor

State Resource Link: https://dphhs.mt.gov/CFSD

Clergy Privilege: Yes. Members of the clergy are not required to make a report if the knowledge came from communication or confession received in their official capacity as a member of the clergy and the communication was intended to be confidential, and the person making the statement does not consent to its disclosure. See Mont. Code Ann. § 41-3-201(6).

Statute of Limitations for Criminal Prosecution

Statutes: Mont. Code § 45-1-205 (2019)

Felonies: Sexual assaults have a ten-year statute of limitations; however, if the victim is less than 18 years old at the time of the crime, then the statute of limitations is twenty years from the eighteenth birthday. Other felonies have a five-year statute of limitations.

Misdemeanors: One year unless a misdemeanor sex offense and victim was under 18 years old, then the statute of limitations is five years from the eighteenth birthday.

DNA Exception: Yes

Statutory Rape / Age of Consent

Statutes: Mont. Code § 45-5-501 through 45-5-503 (2019). By law an individual under the age of 16 years of old is incapable of giving consent for sexual acts. The statutes define the degrees of the crime based on age of victim, age of offender, the difference in age, and relationship between the two.

Age: 16

NEBRASKA

Child Abuse Reporting

Statutes and Regulations: Neb. Rev. Stat. §§ 28-710 through 28-717 (2019)

Who Must Report: Everyone

What Must Be Reported: Physical, sexual, mental abuse, or neglect

Legal Standard: Reasonable Cause to Believe

Penalty for Failure to Report: Misdemeanor

State Resource Link: http://dhhs.ne.gov/Pages/Child-Abuse.aspx

Clergy Privilege: The statues do not address.

Statute of Limitations for Criminal Prosecution

Statutes: Neb. Rev. Stat. § 29-110 (2019)

Felonies: The crimes of first or second degree sexual assault, sexual assault of a child, and incest may be charged at any time, and they do not have statute of limitations. Other felony child abuse crimes have a seven-year statute of limitations or within seven years of the victim's sixteenth birthday whichever is later. Other felonies have a three year statute of limitations.

Misdemeanors: One year to eighteen months.

DNA Exception: No

Statutory Rape / Age of Consent

Statutes: Neb. Rev. Stat. §§ 28-319 through 28.320.01 (2019). The statutes define the degrees of the crime based on age of victim, age of offender, the difference in age, and relationship between the two.

Age: 16

NEVADA

Child Abuse Reporting

Statutes and Regulations: Nev. Rev. Stat. Ann. §§ 432B.010 through 432B.130 (2019) // Nev. Rev. Stat. Ann. §§ 432B.220 through 432B.250 (2019) // Nev. Rev. Stat. Ann. §§ 202.879 through 202.894 (2019)

Who Must Report: Nevada statutes provide a list of mandated reporters which includes *members of the clergy*, medical personnel, mental health providers, social workers, childcare providers, providers of organized activities for children, school employees and volunteers, and law enforcement. Please refer to Nev. Rev. Stat. Ann. § 432B.220 for the complete list of mandated reporters.

What Must Be Reported: Physical abuse, sexual abuse, mental abuse, or neglect by person responsible for the child's welfare. This type of report falls under Nev. Rev. Stat. Ann. § 432B.220.

Any violent or sexual offense against a child under 12 years of age. See Nev. Rev. Stat. Ann. § 202.888 for persons who are exempt from this duty to report.

Legal Standard: Reasonable Cause to Believe is defined by statute as follows: "in light of all the surrounding facts and circumstances which are known or which reasonably should be known to the person at the time, a reasonable person would believe, under those facts and circumstances, that an act, transaction, event, situation or condition exists, is occurring or has occurred." Nev. Rev. Stat. Ann. § 202.879 and §432B.121.

Penalty for Failure to Report: Misdemeanor

State Resource Link: http://dcfs.nv.gov/Programs/CWS/CPS/CPS/

Clergy Privilege: For reports under Nev. Rev. Stat. Ann. § 432B.220, it appears that members of the clergy are prohibited from invoking the privilege. However, for a report under Nev. Rev. Stat. Ann. § 202.888, the privilege appears to exist for communication received in their official capacity.

Statute of Limitations for Criminal Prosecution

Statutes: Nev. Rev. Stat. §§ 171.083 through 171.095 (2019)

Felonies: For the crimes of sexual assault or sex trafficking the statute of limitations is eliminated if a written report is filed with law enforcement officer during the period of limitation—for sex trafficking—4 years; and for sexual assault—20 years. For crimes of child sex abuse or child sex trafficking the charge must be filed before the victim is: (1) Thirty-six years old if the victim discovers or reasonably should have discovered that he or she was a victim of the sexual abuse or sex trafficking by the date on which the victim reaches that age; or (2) Forty-three years old if the victim does not discover and reasonably should not have discovered that he or she was a victim of the sexual abuse or sex trafficking by the date on which the victim reaches 36 years of age. Most other felonies have a three-year statute of limitations.

Misdemeanors: One to two years based on seriousness of misdemeanor

DNA Exception: No

Statutory Rape / Age of Consent

Statutes: Nev. Rev. Stat. §§ 200.364 through 200.368 (2019). In Nevada, it is illegal for a person 18 years old or older to have sexual intercourse, anal intercourse or sexual penetration with a person who is 14 or 15 years of age and who is at least 4 years younger than the perpetrator.

Age: 16

NEW HAMPSHIRE

Child Abuse Reporting

Statutes and Regulations: N.H. Rev. Stat. Ann. § 169-C:3 (2019) // N.H. Rev. Stat. Ann. §§ 169-C:29 through C:39 (2019)

Who Must Report: Everyone

What Must Be Reported: Physical abuse, sexual abuse, mental abuse or neglect

Legal Standard: Reason to Suspect

Penalty for Failure to Report: Misdemeanor

State Resource Link: https://www.dhhs.nh.gov/dcyf/cps/stop.htm

Clergy Privilege: No. See N.H. Rev. Stat. Ann. § 169-C:32.

Statute of Limitations for Criminal Prosecution

Statutes: N.H. Rev. Stat. § 625:8 (2019)

Felonies: For the crime of aggravated sexual assault on a victim under the age of 18, the statute of limitations is twenty-two years from the victim's eighteenth birthday. For sex trafficking, the statute of limitations is twenty years, unless the victim is under the age of 18, and then the statute of limitations is twenty years form the twentieth birthday. For a class A and B felonies the statute of limitations is six years.

Misdemeanors: One year

DNA Exception: No

Statutory Rape / Age of Consent

Statutes: N.H. Rev. Stat. §§ 632-A:2 through A:4 (2019) In New Hampshire, it is illegal to have sexual contact with an individual under the age of 16. A close in age exemption exists for parties who are less than 3 years apart, and only when the younger party is older than 13 but younger than 16. However, if the offender holds a position of authority over the victim the age of consent raises to 18 years of age.

Age: 16

NEW JERSEY

Child Abuse Reporting

Statutes and Regulations: N.J. Stat. Ann §§ 9:6-8.9; 9:6-8.10; 9:6-8.14 (2019)

Who Must Report: Everyone

What Must Be Reported: Physical, sexual, or mental abuse or neglect by child's parent, guardian, or other person having custody and control.

Legal Standard: Reasonable Cause to Believe

Penalty for Failure to Report: Deemed a "Disorderly Person."

State Resource Link: https://www.state.nj.us/dcf/reporting/how/index.html

Clergy Privilege: The statutes do not address.

Statute of Limitations for Criminal Prosecution

Statutes: N.J. Stat. § 2C:1-6 (2019)

Felonies: The crime of aggravated sexual assaults may be filed at any time and does not have a statute of limitations. For sexual contact with a minor, the charge must be brought within five years of the victim reaching 18 years of age. Most other felonies have a five-year statute of limitations.

Misdemeanors: One year

DNA Exception: Yes

Statutory Rape / Age of Consent

Statutes: N.J. Stat. § 2C:14-2 (2019). New Jersey prohibits an individual from having sexual intercourse with anyone under the age of 16. A close in age exemption exists allowing minors between ages 13 and 15 to engage in sexual activity with a partner up to 4 years older. If the offender is a parent, guardian, sibling, a relative closer than a 4th cousin, or an individual with some authority over the victim, then the age of consent raises to 18 years of age.

Age: 16

NEW MEXICO

Child Abuse Reporting

Statutes and Regulations: N.M. Stat. Ann. §§ 32A-4-2 through 32A-4-3 (2019)

Who Must Report: Everyone

What Must Be Reported: Physical, sexual, or mental abuse or neglect by child's parent, guardian, or custodian.

Legal Standard: Reasonable Suspicion

Penalty for Failure to Report: Misdemeanor

State Resource Link: https://cyfd.org/child-abuse-neglect/reporting-abuse-or-neglect/

Clergy Privilege: Yes. However, a member of the clergy who has information that is not privileged as a matter of law is required to report. See N.M. Stat. Ann. § 32A-4-3(A).

Statute of Limitations for Criminal Prosecution

Statutes: N.M. Stat. §§ 30-1-8 through 30-1-9.2 (2019). Felonies: First degree violent felonies may be brought at any time and do not have a statute of limitations. For the crimes of sexual penetration and sexual contact against a child the statute of limitations does not begin to run until the child is 18 years old or the crimes is reported to law enforcement, whichever happens first. Other felonies have a statute of limitations that varies between five and six years.

Misdemeanors: Two years

DNA Exception: Yes

Statutory Rape / Age of Consent

Statutes: N.M. Stat. §§ 30-9-11 30-9-13 (2019) In New Mexico, a person who is 18 years old or older is prohibited from having sexual intercourse with anyone under the age of seventeen who is at least 4 years younger whom they are not married to. If the offender is a school employee, then the age of consent is raised to 18 year old.

Age: 17

NEW YORK

Child Abuse Reporting

Statutes and Regulations: N.Y. Soc. Serv. Law §§ 412 through (2019)

Who Must Report: New York statutes provide a list of mandated reporters which includes medical personnel, mental health providers, social workers, childcare providers, camps, school employees, and law enforcement. Please refer to N.Y. Soc. Serv. Law § 413 for the complete list of mandated reporters.

What Must Be Reported: Physical abuse, mental abuse, sexual abuse, or neglect.

Legal Standard: Reasonable Cause to Suspect

Penalty for Failure to Report: Misdemeanor and civil liability.

State Resource Link: https://ocfs.ny.gov/main/cps/

Clergy Privilege: The statutes do not address.

Statute of Limitations for Criminal Prosecution

Statutes: N.Y. Crim. Proc. Law § 30.10 (2019)

Felonies: First degree rape, first degree aggravated sexual abuse, or first degree sexual conduct against a child may be commenced at any time and do not have a statute of limitations. A prosecution for any other felony must be commenced within five years after the commission of the crime.

Misdemeanors: Two years

DNA Exception: Yes

Statutory Rape / Age of Consent

Statutes: N.Y. Penal Law § 130.05, §§ 130.25 through 130.50. By law an individual under the age of 17 years of old is incapable of giving consent for sexual acts. The statutes define the degrees of the crime based on age of victim, age of offender, the difference in age, and relationship between the two.

Age: 17

NORTH CAROLINA

Child Abuse Reporting

Statutes and Regulations: N.C. Gen Stat. § 7B-101 (2019)   //   N.C. Gen Stat. §§ 7B-301 through 7B-310 (2019)

Who Must Report: Everyone

What Must Be Reported: Physical abuse, mental abuse, neglect, or dependency by a parent, guardian, custodian, or caretaker.

Human trafficking by anyone.

Legal Standard: Cause to Suspect

Penalty for Failure to Report: Misdemeanor

State Resource Link: https://www.ncdhhs.gov/divisions/social-services/child-welfare-services/child-protective-services

Clergy Privilege: No. See N.C. Gen Stat. §§ 7B-310.

Statute of Limitations for Criminal Prosecution

Case Law: *State v. Hardin*, 201 S.E.2d 74 (N.C. Ct. App. 1973).

Felonies: In North Carolina, felony crimes may be filed at any time and do not have a statute of limitations.

Misdemeanors: Two years

DNA Exception: No

Statutory Rape / Age of Consent

Statutes: N.C. Gen Stat. §§ 14-27.23 through 14-32. (2019). In North Carolina, it is illegal for an individual to engage in sexual intercourse with an individual under the age of 16. A close in age exemption exists of four years. A school employee is prohibited from having sexual contact with any student at the school, and a person acting in the role of parent is prohibited from engaging in sexual conduct with their child.

Age: 16

NORTH DAKOTA

Child Abuse Reporting

Statutes and Regulations: N.D. Cent. Code §§ 50-25.1.02 through (2019)

Who Must Report: North Dakota statutes provide a list of mandated reporters which includes *members of the clergy*, medical personnel, mental health providers, social workers, childcare providers, school employees, and law enforcement. Please refer to N.D. Cent. Code §§ 50-25.1.03(1) for the complete list of mandated reporters.

Everyone who has knowledge based on images of sexual conduct by a child discovered on a workplace computer

What Must Be Reported: Physical abuse, mental abuse, or neglect by one responsible for child's welfare (parent, guardian, foster parent, school employee, child care facility employee, or person responsible for care in residential setting)

Sexual abuse committed by anyone.

Legal Standard: Reasonable Cause to Suspect

Penalty for Failure to Report: Misdemeanor

State Resource Link: https://www.nd.gov/dhs/services/childfamily/cps/#mandating

Clergy Privilege: Yes. Members of the clergy are "not required to report such circumstances if the knowledge or suspicion is derived from information received in the capacity of spiritual adviser." See N.D. Cent. Code § 50-25.1-03(1).

Statute of Limitations for Criminal Prosecution

Statutes: N.D. Cent. Code §§ 29-04-02 through 29-04-03.1 (2019)

Felonies: In North Dakota, crimes of gross sexual imposition or human trafficking have a seven year statute of limitations. Prosecutions of sex crimes against minors have a ten-year statute of limitations, but if the minor victim did not report then it is three years from the report date. All other felonies have a statute of limitations of three years.

Misdemeanors: Two years

DNA Exception: Yes

Statutory Rape / Age of Consent

Statutes: N.D. Cent. Code §§ 12.1-2—01 though 12.1-20-08 (2019). In North Dakota, it is illegal to have sexual contact with a person under the age of 18. There is a close in age exemption of three years, but this does not apply if the offender is an adult or is in a parental role.

Age: 18

OHIO

Child Abuse Reporting

Statutes and Regulations: Ohio Rev. Code Ann. §§ 2151.011 through 2151.05 (2019) // Ohio Rev. Code Ann. §§ 2151.421 (2019)

Who Must Report: Ohio statutes provide a list of mandated reporters which includes *members of the clergy*, medical personnel, mental health providers, social workers, childcare providers, school employees, camp employees, person, other than a cleric, rendering spiritual treatment through prayer in accordance with the tenets of a well-recognized religion and law enforcement. Please refer to Ohio Rev. Code Ann. §§ 2151.421.

What Must Be Reported: Physical abuse or sexual abuse committed by anyone, and mental abuse or neglect by parent, guardian, or custodian.

Abuse by clergy

Legal Standard: Reasonable Cause to Suspect

Penalty for Failure to Report: Misdemeanor

State Resource Link: https://jfs.ohio.gov/ocf/reportchildabuseandneglect.stm

Clergy Privilege: Yes. Members of the clergy are not mandated to report communication received as penitent within the "cleric-penitent relationship." However, Members of the clergy shall make a report if all of the following apply "the penitent, at the time of the communication, is a child under eighteen years of age or is a person under twenty-one years of age with a developmental disability or physical impairment; the cleric knows, or has reasonable cause to believe based on facts that would cause a reasonable person in a similar position to believe, as a result of the communication or any observations made during that communication, the penitent has suffered or faces a threat of suffering any physical or mental wound, injury, disability, or condition of a nature that reasonably indicates abuse or neglect of the penitent; the abuse or neglect does not arise out of the penitent's attempt to have an abortion performed upon a child under eighteen years of age or upon a person under twenty-one years of age with a developmental disability or physical impairment without the notification of her parents, guardian, or custodian." See Ohio Rev. Code Ann. §§ 2151.421.

Statute of Limitations for Criminal Prosecution

Statutes: Ohio Rev. Code Ann. § 2901.13 (2019)

Felonies: For the crimes of rape and sexual battery, the statute of limitations is twenty-five years. For sexual conduct with a minor, other sex crimes, and gross sexual imposition, the statute of limitations is twenty years. When the victim is a minor the twenty years starts running when the victim turns 18 or from the point that authorities were notified. All other felonies have a statute of limitations of six years.

Misdemeanors: Six months to two years depending on seriousness of offense.

DNA Exception: Yes

Statutory Rape / Age of Consent

Statutes: Ohio Rev. Code Ann. § 2907.04 (2019) In Ohio, it is illegal to have sexual intercourse with an individual under the age of 16. A close-in-age exemption exists allowing minors aged 13 and older to consent to an individual under the age of 18.

Age: 16

OKLAHOMA

Child Abuse Reporting

Statutes and Regulations: Okla. Stat Ann. tit. 10A § 1-1-105 (2019) // Okla. Stat Ann. tit. 10A §§ 1-2-101 (2019)

Who Must Report: Everyone

What Must Be Reported: Physical, sexual, or mental abuse or neglect by a person responsible for the child's welfare—parent; legal guardian; custodian; foster parent; employee of a child care facility.

Legal Standard: Reason to Believe

Penalty for Failure to Report: Misdemeanor

State Resource Link: https://www.ok.gov/health2/documents/Child%20Abuse%20 Hotline%20Card%20English%202017.pdf

Clergy Privilege: No. Privilege does not relieve duty to report under this section.

Statute of Limitations for Criminal Prosecution

Statutes: Okla. Stat. tit. 22, § 152 (2019)

Felonies: Sex crimes perpetrated against children must be brought before the victim's forty-fifth birthday. Sex crimes perpetrated against those over the age of 18 have a statute of limitations of twelve years from the time of notification to law enforcement.

Misdemeanors: Three years

DNA Exception: Yes

Statutory Rape / Age of Consent

Statutes: Okla. Stat. tit. 21, §§ 1111 and 1112 (2019). In Oklahoma, it is illegal for an individual to have sexual intercourse with an individual under the age of 16. A close-in-age exemption allows minors over age 14 to consent to an individual younger than 18 years old. In addition, the age of consent raises to 18 years old if the offender is in a school supervisory role over the victim or is responsible for their welfare.

Age: 16

OREGON

Child Abuse Reporting

Statutes and Regulations: Or. Rev. Stat. §§ 419B.05 through 419B.010 (2019)

Who Must Report: Oregon statutes make all "public and private officials" mandated reporters. A list of public or private officials includes *members of the clergy*, medical personnel, mental health providers, social workers, childcare providers, school employees, coaches, camps and scouting programs, and law enforcement. Please refer to Or. Rev. Stat. § 419B.005 for the complete list of mandated reporters.

What Must Be Reported: Physical abuse, sexual abuse, or mental abuse or neglect.

Legal Standard: Reasonable Cause to Believe

Penalty for Failure to Report: Class A Violation

State Resource Link: https://www.oregon.gov/DHS/ABUSE/Pages/mandatory_report.aspx

Clergy/Parishioner Privilege: Yes. Members of the clergy are not required to report information that was communicated in a privileged capacity. See Or. Rev. Stat § 419B.010.

Statute of Limitations for Criminal Prosecution

Statutes: Or. Rev. Stat. §§ 131.125 (2019)

Felonies: The crimes of first degree rape, sodomy, first degree unlawful sexual penetration, and first-degree sex abuse have a statute of limitations of twelve years. However, if the victim was a minor at the time of the crime, the charges must be brought before the victim reaches the age of thirty. All of other sexual crimes have a statute of limitations of six years, except for when the victim was under the age of 18 at time of crime, the charges must be commenced by the victim's thirtieth birthday or within twelve years of the report to law enforcement whichever occurs first.

Misdemeanors: Two years is the general statute of limitations for misdemeanors; however, misdemeanor abuse crimes against those under the age of eighteen, have a statute of limitations of either four years from the report to law enforcement of the victim's twenty-second birthday whichever comes first.

DNA Exception: Yes

Statutory Rape / Age of Consent

Statutes: Or. Rev. Stat. §§163.315 through 163.375 (2019). In Oregon, it is illegal to have sexual contact with an individual under the age of 18. A close-in-age exemption allows minors to consent to an individual that is less than three years older.

Age: 18

PENNSYLVANIA

Child Abuse Reporting

Statutes and Regulations: 23 Pa. Cons. Stat. §§ 6303 through 6319 (2019)

Who Must Report: Pennsylvania statutes provide a list of mandated reporters which includes *members of the clergy,* medical personnel, mental health providers, social workers, childcare providers, school employees, and law enforcement. Please refer to 23 Pa. Cons. Stat. § 6311for the complete list of mandated reporters.

What Must Be Reported: Physical, mental, or sexual abuse, or neglect by a parent, spouse, former spouse of parent, paramour of parent, person 18 years old or older who is related, person engaged in trafficking, person 14 years old or older who resides in home, person 14 years old or older who is responsible for care of child or has direct contact through child care services, school, program, activity, or service.

Legal Standard: Reasonable Cause to Suspect

Penalty for Failure to Report: Felony or Misdemeanor

State Resource Link: https://www.compass.state.pa.us/compass.web/Public/CMPHome

Clergy Privilege: Yes. Confidential communications made to a member of the clergy are protected under 42 Pa. Cons. Stat. § 5943. See also 23 Pa. Cons. Stat. § 6311.1(b).

Statute of Limitations for Criminal Prosecution

Statutes: 42 Pa. Cons. Stat. § 5552 (2019)

Felonies: The statute of limitations for major sex offenses is twelve years. However, for sexual offenses committed against a minor, the charge may be filed up until the minor reaches the age of 50.

Misdemeanors: Two years

DNA Exception: Yes

Statutory Rape / Age of Consent

Statutes: 18 Pa. Cons. Stat. §§ 3121 through 31 (2019) // 18 Pa. Cons. Stat. § 6301(2019). In Pennsylvania, it is illegal to have sexual contact with an individual under the age of 16; however, there is a corruption of minors statute that sets the age at 18. So, the laws are in conflict. The laws may allow individuals aged 16 or 17 to consent to each other, but not to anyone 18 or older. Individuals between 13 and 15 may or may not be able to consent to someone less than four years older, because while they might not be affected by the statutory rape laws, they could be prosecuted under other statutes.

Age: 16 (possibly 18).

RHODE ISLAND

Child Abuse Reporting

Statutes and Regulations: R.I. Gen. Laws §§ 40-11-1 through 40-11-11 (2019)

Who Must Report: Everyone

What Must Be Reported: Physical, sexual, or mental abuse by a person responsible for child's welfare includes parent, guardian, foster parent, or child care worker.

Sexual abuse by employee, agent, contractor, or volunteer of an educational program.

Legal Standard: Reasonable Cause to Suspect

Penalty for Failure to Report: Misdemeanor

State Resource Link: http://www.dcyf.ri.gov/child-protective-services/

Clergy Privilege: No. See R.I. Gen. Laws § 40-11-11.

Statute of Limitations for Criminal Prosecution

Statutes: R.I. Gen. Laws § 12-12-17 (2019)

Felonies: The crimes of rape, first-degree sexual assault, first-degree child molestation sexual assault, second-degree child molestation sexual assault, bigamy may be brought at any time and do not have a statute of limitations. Other felonies have a three years statute of limitations.

Misdemeanors: Three years

DNA Exception: No

Statutory Rape / Age of Consent

Statutes: R.I. Gen. Laws § 11-37-6 (2019). In Rhode Island, it is against the law to have sexual intercourse with an individual under the age of 16.

Age: 16

SOUTH CAROLINA

Child Abuse Reporting

Statutes and Regulations: S.C. Code Ann. §§ 63-7-20 through 63-7-310 (2019)

Who Must Report: South Carolina statutes provide a list of mandated reporters which includes *members of the clergy*, medical personnel, mental health providers, social workers, childcare providers, school employees, and law enforcement. Please refer to S.C. Code Ann. §63-7-310 for the complete list of mandated reporters.

What Must Be Reported: Physical, sexual, or mental abuse or neglect by a child's "parent, guardian or other person responsible for his welfare" (includes an employee of a child day care facility),

If child is a victim of trafficking.

Legal Standard: Reason to Believe

Penalty for Failure to Report: Misdemeanor

State Resource Link: https://dss.sc.gov/abuseneglect/report-child-abuse-and-neglect/

Clergy Privilege: Yes. However, "a clergy member . . . *must report* in accordance with this sub-article except when information is received from the alleged perpetrator of the abuse and neglect during a communication that is protected by the clergy and penitent privilege." See S.C. Code Ann. § 19-11-90 and § 63-7-420.

Statute of Limitations for Criminal Prosecution

In South Carolina, there is no statute of limitations for criminal offenses.

Statutory Rape / Age of Consent

Statutes: S.C. Code Ann. § 16-3-655 (2019). In South Carolina, it is illegal to have sexual contact with an individual who is under the age of sixteen. There are no close-in-age exemptions at this time.

Age: 16

SOUTH DAKOTA

Child Abuse Reporting

Statutes and Regulations: S.D. Codified Laws §§ 26-8A-2 through 26-8A-8 (2019)

Who Must Report: South Dakota statutes provide a list of mandated reporters which includes medical personnel, mental health providers, social workers, childcare providers, school employees, and law enforcement. Please refer to S.D. Codified Laws § 26-8A-3 for the complete list of mandated reporters.

What Must Be Reported: Physical or mental abuse or neglect by parent, guardian, or custodian.

Sexual abuse by parent, guardian, custodian or other person responsible for child's care.

Legal Standard: Reasonable Cause to Suspect

Penalty for Failure to Report: Misdemeanor

State Resource Link: https://apps.sd.gov/SS60ReporterVideoTraining/Introduction.aspx

Clergy Privilege: The statutes do not address.

Statute of Limitations for Criminal Prosecution

Statutes: S.D. Codified Laws § 22-22-1 and § 23A-42-2 (2019)

Felonies: Charges for first and second degree rape may be commenced at any time and do not have a statute of limitations. For all other felonies, the statute of limitations is seven years. Specifically, for third and fourth degree rape, when the victim was a minor, the statute of limitations is seven years or before the victim turns twenty-five, whichever is later.

Misdemeanors: Seven years

DNA Exception: No

Statutory Rape / Age of Consent

Statutes: S.D. Codified Laws §§ 22-22-1 through 22-22-7.3 (2019). In South Dakota, it is illegal to have sexual intercourse with an individual under the age of 16. There is no close-in-age exemption; however, the difference in age may affect the severity of the punishment.

Age: 16

TENNESSEE

Child Abuse Reporting

Statutes and Regulations: Tenn. Code Ann. §§ 37-1-102 (2019) // Tenn. Code Ann. §§ 37-1-401 through 37-1-412 (2019) // Tenn. Code Ann. §§ 37-1-601 through 37-1-615 (2019)

Who Must Report: Everyone

What Must Be Reported: Physical, mental, or sexual abuse, or neglect by parent guardian or caretaker.

Sexual abuse by anyone.

Legal Standard: Reasonable Cause to Suspect

Penalty for Failure to Report: Misdemeanor

State Resource Link: https://www.tn.gov/dcs/program-areas/child-safety/reporting.html

Clergy Privilege: Yes. However, the privilege "shall not apply to any situation involving known or suspected child sexual abuse and shall not constitute grounds for failure to report as required by this part, failure to cooperate with the department in its activities pursuant to this part, or failure to give evidence in any judicial proceeding relating to child sexual abuse." See Tenn. Code Ann. § 37-1-614.

Statute of Limitations for Criminal Prosecution

Statutes: Tenn. Code § 40-2-101 and § 40-2-102 (2019)

Felonies: the crime of aggravated rape has a statute of limitations of fifteen years. Other degrees of rape and aggravated sexual battery have a statute of limitations of eight years. AS for sexual crimes perpetrated against minor victims, please see the statutes to determine the statute of limitations because the limitation varies based on when the crime was committed.

Misdemeanors: One year

DNA Exception: Possibly allowed by case law.

Statutory Rape / Age of Consent

Statutes: Tenn. Code §§ 39-13-501 through and §39-13-509 (2019). In Tennessee, it is illegal to have sexual intercourse with an individual under the age of 18. A close-in age-exemption exists which allows individuals between the ages of 13 and 18 years of age to consent in situations where the other person is less than 4 years older.

Age: 18

TEXAS

Child Abuse Reporting

Statutes and Regulations: Tex. Fam. Code Ann. § 261-001 (2019) // Tex. Fam. Code Ann. §§ 261-101 through 261-109 (2019)

Who Must Report: Everyone

What Must Be Reported: Physical, mental, or sexual abuse or neglect.

Legal Standard: Cause to Believe

Penalty for Failure to Report: Misdemeanor

State Resource Link: https://www.dfps.state.tx.us/Contact_Us/report_abuse.asp

Clergy Privilege: No. "The requirement to report under this section applies without exception to an individual whose personal communications may otherwise be privileged, . . . a member of the clergy." See Tex. Fam. Code Ann. § 261.101(c).

Statute of Limitations for Criminal Prosecution

Statutes: Tex. Code Crim. Proc. art. 12.01 (2019)

Felonies: The crimes of felony aggravated sexual assault, continuous sexual abuse of child, indecency with a child, and trafficking may be commenced at any time and do not have a statute of limitations. For other sexual assaults there is a ten-year statute of limitations. There are a number of other charges that minors with varying statutes of limitations. General felonies have a three statute of limitations.

Misdemeanors: Two years

DNA Exception: Yes

Statutory Rape / Age of Consent

Statutes: Tex. Penal. Code Ann. §§ 21.11 through 21.12 (2019). In Texas, it is illegal to engages in sexual contact with an individual under the age of 17. A close-in-age exemption exists that allows for minors to consent to sexual contact with someone that is no more than three years older than the victim.

Age: 17

UTAH

Child Abuse Reporting

Statutes and Regulations: Utah Code Ann. §§ 62A-4a-402 through 411 (2019)

Who Must Report: Everyone

What Must Be Reported: Physical, sexual, or mental abuse or neglect.

Legal Standard: Reasonable Cause to Believe

Penalty for Failure to Report: Misdemeanor

State Resource Link: https://pcautah.org and https://dcfs.utah.gov/services/child-protective-services/

Clergy Privilege: Yes. The requirement to report "does not apply to a member of the clergy, with regard to any confession made to the member of the clergy while functioning in the ministerial capacity of the member of the clergy and without the consent of the individual making the confession, if:

> **(a)** the perpetrator made the confession directly to the member of the clergy; and **(b)** the member of the clergy is, under canon law or church doctrine or practice, bound to maintain the confidentiality of that confession." *However*, "when a member of the clergy receives information about abuse or neglect from any source other than confession of the perpetrator, the member of the clergy is required to report that information even though the member of the clergy may have also received information about abuse or neglect from the confession of the perpetrator." In addition, even if the clergy member is exempt, it "does not exempt the member of the clergy from any other efforts required by law to prevent further abuse or neglect by the perpetrator." See Utah Code Ann. § 62A-4a-403.

Statute of Limitations for Criminal Prosecution

Statutes: Utah Code Ann. §§ 76-1-301 through 76-1-302 (2019)

Felonies: The crimes of rape; rape of a child; object rape; object rape of a child; forcible sodomy; sodomy on a child; sexual abuse of a child; aggravated sexual abuse of a child; aggravated sexual assault; aggravated human trafficking or aggravated human smuggling may be commenced at any time and do not have a statute of limitations. For other felony abuse crimes, the statute of limitations varies from four years to eight years.

Misdemeanors: Two years

DNA Exception: Yes

Statutory Rape / Age of Consent

Statutes: Utah Code Ann. §§ 76-5-401 through 76-5-401.3 (2019). In Utah, it is illegal to have sexual intercourse with an individual under the age of 18. A close-in-age exemptions exists which allows for individuals who are 16 and 17 years old to consent in situations where the other person is less than 7 years older.

Age: 18

VERMONT

Child Abuse Reporting

Statutes and Regulations: Vt. Stat. Ann. tit 33 §§ 4911 through 4913 (2019)

Who Must Report: Vermont statutes provide a list of mandated reporters which includes *members of the clergy*, medical personnel, mental health providers, social workers, childcare providers, school employees, camp personnel, and law enforcement. Please refer to Vt. Stat. Ann. tit 33 § 4913 for the complete list of mandated reporters.

What Must Be Reported: Physical abuse, mental abuse, or neglect by parent or other person responsible for child's welfare.

Sexual abuse by any person.

Legal Standard: Reasonable Suspicion

Penalty for Failure to Report: Misdemeanor

State Resource Link: https://dcf.vermont.gov/protection/reporting

Clergy Privilege: Yes. "A member of the clergy shall not be required to make a report under this section if the report would be based upon information received in a communication which is made to a member of the clergy acting in his or her capacity as spiritual advisor; intended by the parties to be confidential at the time the communication is made; intended by the communicant to be an act of contrition or a matter of conscience; and required to be confidential by religious law, doctrine, or tenet." However, if a member of the clergy "receives information about abuse or neglect of a child in a manner other than as described [above], he or she is required to report on the basis of that information even though he or she may have also received a report of abuse or neglect about the same person or incident in the manner described [above]." Vt. Stat. Ann. tit 33 § 4913(j) and (k).

Statute of Limitations for Criminal Prosecution

Statutes: Vt. Stat. Ann. tit.13, § 4501 (2019)

Felonies: Charges for the crimes of aggravated sexual assault, aggravated sexual assault of a child, sexual assault, human trafficking, aggravated human trafficking may be commenced at any time and do not have a statute of limitations. For the crimes of lewd and lascivious conduct against a child and sexual exploitation of a minor, those charges have a statute of limitations of forty years. Most other felonies have a three-year statute of limitations.

Misdemeanors: Three years

DNA Exception: No

Statutory Rape / Age of Consent

Statutes: Vt. Stat. Ann. tit.13, § 3252 (2019). In Vermont, it is illegal to engage in sexual acts with an individual who is under the age of 16. There are some exemptions to this based on age difference. The age of consent is raised to 18 years of age if the offender is related to or is in a position of authority over the victim.

Age: 16

VIRGINIA

Child Abuse Reporting

Statutes and Regulations: Va. Code Ann. § 63.2-1501 (2019) // Va. Code Ann. §§ 63.2-1508 through 1510 (2019)

Who Must Report: Virginia statutes provide a list of mandated reporters which includes medical personnel, mental health providers, social workers, childcare providers, school employees, coaches, camp personnel, and law enforcement. Please refer to Va. Code Ann. § 63.2-1509 for the complete list of mandated reporters.

Enacted 3/18/19: 19. Any minister, priest, rabbi, imam, or duly accredited practitioner of any religious organization or denomination usually referred to as a church as it relates to (i) information, unless the information supporting the suspicion of child abuse or neglect (i) is required by the doctrine of the religious organization or denomination to be kept in a confidential manner or (ii) information that would be subject to Section 8.01-400 or 19.2-271.3 if offered as evidence in court.

What Must Be Reported: Physical, sexual, or mental abuse or neglect by parent or other caretaker.

Legal Standard: Reason to Suspect

Penalty for Failure to Report: Fine of $500

State Resource Link: http://www.dss.virginia.gov/family/cps/index.cgi

Clergy Privilege: Yes. Members of the clergy not required to report if . . .

Statute of Limitations for Criminal Prosecution

Statute and Case Law: Va. Code § 19.2-8 (2019); *Foster v. Virginia,* 606 S.E. 2d 518, (Va. Ct. App. 2004)

Felonies: In Virginia there is no statute of limitations for felonies.

Misdemeanors: One year

DNA Exception: No

Statutory Rape / Age of Consent

Statutes: Va. Code § 18.2-6; § 18.2-63; and § 18.2-371 (2019). In Virginia, it is illegal for an individual to "carnally know" or engage in sexual activity with an individual under the age of 18.

Age: 18

WASHINGTON

Child Abuse Reporting

Statutes and Regulations: Wash. Rev. Code §§ 26.44.010 through 26.44.80 (2019)

Who Must Report: Washington statutes provide a list of mandated reporters which includes medical personnel, mental health providers, social workers, childcare providers, school employees, and law enforcement. Please refer to Wash. Rev. Code § 26.44.030 for the complete list of mandated reporters.

What Must Be Reported: Physical, mental, or sexual abuse or neglect by anyone.

Legal Standard: Reasonable Cause to Believe: By statute, reasonable cause to believe means "a person witnesses or receives a credible written or oral report alleging abuse, including sexual contact, or neglect of a child." Wash. Rev. Code § 26.44.030(1)(b) (iii).

Penalty for Failure to Report: Gross Misdemeanor

State Resource Link: https://www.dcyf.wa.gov/safety/report-abuse

Clergy Privilege: Yes. Members of the clergy are not subject to the reporting requirements of this statute. See *State v. Motherwell*, 788 P.2d 1066 (Wash. 1990).

Statute of Limitations for Criminal Prosecution

Statutes: Wash. Rev. Code § 9A.04.080 (2019)

Felonies: The crimes of indent liberties and some rapes have a statute of limitations of ten years (if rapes were reported within one year of the commission, otherwise only a three year statute of limitations). Many child sex crimes may be prosecuted up to the victim's thirtieth birthday. Generally, the statute of limitations for felonies is three years.

Misdemeanors: One to two years

DNA Exception: Yes

Statutory Rape / Age of Consent

Statutes: Wash. Rev. Code §§ 9A.44.073 through 9A.44.100 (2019). In Washington, it is illegal for an individual to engage in sexual activity with an individual under the age of 16. There is a close-in-age exemption if the offender is less than four years older than the victim.

Age: 16

WEST VIRGINIA

Child Abuse Reporting

Statutes and Regulations: W. Va. Code Ann. §§ 49-2-801 through 49-2-812 (2019)

Who Must Report: West Virginia statutes provide a list of mandated reporters which includes *members of the clergy*, medical personnel, mental health providers, social workers, childcare providers, school employees, camp personnel, and law enforcement. Please refer to W. Va. Code Ann. § 49-2-803 for the complete list of mandated reporters.

What Must Be Reported: Physical, mental, or sexual abuse or neglect.

Legal Standard: Reasonable Cause to Suspect

Penalty for Failure to Report: Misdemeanor

State Resource Link: https://dhhr.wv.gov/bcf/Pages/Search.aspx?q=Centralized%20 Intake

Clergy Privilege: No. See W. Va. Code Ann. § 49-2-803.

Statute of Limitations for Criminal Prosecution

Case Law: *State v. Carrico*, 427 S.E. 2d 474, 477 (W. Va. 1993)

Felonies: In West Virginia, felonies do not have a statute if limitations.

Misdemeanors: One year

DNA Exception: No

Statutory Rape / Age of Consent

Statutes: W. Va. Code Ann. §§ 61-8B-2 through 61-8B-9 (2019). In West Virginia, an individual who is less than sixteen years old is incapable of giving consent. Therefore, it is illegal to engage in sexual activity with an individual who is under the age of 16. A close-in-age exemption exists if the as long the offender is not more than 4 years older.

Age: 16

WISCONSIN

Child Abuse Reporting

Statutes and Regulations: Wis. Stat. §§ 48.981 (2019)

Who Must Report: Wisconsin statutes provide a list of mandated reporters which includes *members of the clergy,* medical personnel, mental health providers, social workers, childcare providers, school employees, and law enforcement. Please refer to Wis. Stat. § 48.981 for the complete list of mandated reporters.

What Must Be Reported: Physical, sexual, or mental abuse or neglect. Abuse of child by member of the clergy must be reported by members of the clergy pursuant to Wis. Stat. § 48.981(2)(bm).

Legal Standard: Reasonable Cause to Suspect

Penalty for Failure to Report: Fine or imprisonment

State Resource Link: https://dcf.wisconsin.gov/cps/mandatedreporters

Clergy Privilege: Yes. Members of the clergy are not subject to the requirements of the reporting statutes if the information was received "solely through confidential communications made to him or her privately or in a confessional setting if he or she is authorized to hear or is accustomed to hearing such communications and, under the disciplines, tenets, or traditions of his or her religion, has a duty or is expected to keep those communications secret." See Wis. Stat. § 48.981(2)(bm)(3).

Statute of Limitations for Criminal Prosecution

Statutes: Wis. Stat. § 939.74 (2019)

Felonies: Charges for sexual assault and sexual assault of a child may be commenced at any time and do not have a statute of limitations. Other sexual crimes committed against minors must v=be commenced by the victim's forty-fifth birthday. Other felonies have a six year statute of limitations.

Misdemeanors: Three years

DNA Exception: Yes

Statutory Rape / Age of Consent

Statutes: Wis. Stat. §§ 948.01 through 948.093 (2019). In Wisconsin, it is illegal to engage in sexual activity with an individual who is under the age of 18.

Age: 18

WYOMING

Child Abuse Reporting

Statutes and Regulations: Wyo. Stat. Ann. §§ 14-3-201 through 14-3-210 (2019)

Who Must Report: Everyone

What Must Be Reported: Physical, sexual or mental abuse or neglect.

Legal Standard: Reasonable Cause to Suspect

Penalty for Failure to Report: Misdemeanor

State Resource Link: http://dfsweb.wyo.gov/social-services/mandatory-reporting

Clergy Privilege: Yes. Members of the clergy are not required to report regarding information "concerning a confession made to him in his professional character if enjoined by the church to which he belongs." Wyo. Stat. Ann. § 1-12-101 and § 14-3-210.

Statute of Limitations for Criminal Prosecution

Statutes: Remmick v. State, 275 P. 3d 467, 470 (Wyo. 2012)

Felonies: In Wyoming, felonies do not have a statute of limitations.

Misdemeanors: None

DNA Exception: No

Statutory Rape / Age of Consent

Statutes: Wyo. Stat. Ann. §§ 6-2-303 through 6-2-317 (2019). In Wyoming, it is illegal to engage in sexual activity with an individual who is under the age of 17. The age of consent is raised to 18 years old if the offender is in a position of authority in relation to the victim.

Age: 17

Appendix B

Question: Which leaders in our church or ministry need to review each lesson?

Paid Staff

- All lessons (entire curriculum)

Lay Leaders

Every leader:
- Lessons 1 and 2

Children and Youth/Student Ministry Leaders (i.e. child care volunteers, mission trip leaders, VBS leaders, AWANA):
- Lessons 3, 7, and 9

Deacons and Elders:
- Lessons 1, 2, and 9

Women's Discipleship Coordinator:
- Lessons 6, 8, and 9

Marriage Ministry Leaders:
- Lessons 6 and 8

Men's Ministry Leaders:
- Lessons 6 and 8

Purity Ministry (i.e., pornography):
- Lessons 5, 6, 7, 8, and 10

Recovery Ministries (i.e., Celebrate Recovery, 12-step programs)
- Lessons 6, 8, and 10

Community Outreach Ministries (i.e., ESL, childcare workers):
- Lesson 7

Mission Organizations (i.e., IMB)
- All lessons (entire curriculum)